DEA.

GONE TO POT

Welcome to the Shit Show:

7 Dirty Little Secrets of the Cannabis Industry

A Cannabis Industry Insider's Perspective

FOREWORD BY BILL SNOW

AUTHOR OF *Mergers & Acquisitions For Dummies*

GONE TO POT

DEAN K. MATT

GONE TO POT

Welcome to the Shit Show:
7 Dirty Little Secrets of the Cannabis Industry

A Cannabis Industry Insider's Perspective

MuchoDeanAero

Naperville, Illinois

GONE TO POT may be purchased for educational, business, or sales
promotional use. For further information about special discounts for bulk
purchases, please contact sales@golfgear.golf.

First edition published 2020 by Golf Gear, LLC, dba MuchoDeanAero
Naperville, Illinois

Cover and Book Design by BookBaby

Printed in the United States of America

DISCLAIMER: Any application of the material set forth in the following
pages is at the reader's discretion and is his or her sole responsibility.

Library of Congress Control Number 2019920270

ISBN (paperback) 978-1-54399-857-3

ISBN (eBook) 978-1-54399-858-0

https://gonetopotbook.com

To my family who lived this year-long pursuit of the latest shiny object — the cannabis industry — and who knows, first-hand, how this movie ends.

Contents

Foreword

"The caravan" was a term I heard throughout my childhood, my teen years, and well into my adult years. It was a term my father used to describe the phenomena that seems to infect the investment and business world every few years. My father was a CFO and as I proudly tell anyone who will listen, a self-made man who did not come from means. He put himself through college by digging ditches and advanced by virtue of his wits, honesty, and willingness to outwork everyone. After a successful career, which included taking numerous companies public, he retired and split time between two homes, both on golf courses, quietly helped others, donated more than his fair share to good causes, and bragged that he never lost money on investments.

My father passed away in 2017. After he died, I spoke with the professional who managed his money for nearly four decades and learned something I never knew about my own father: He never owned stock in a company unless he was an employee. That wasn't a total surprise to me. My father was street smart, intimidating, and a skeptic. He had an exquisite bullshit detector and was loath to trust others, especially where his finances were concerned. He was careful with what he earned and while a point can be made that he perhaps lost out on some upside, he never suffered downside losses. His criteria were liquidity, income, and security. Other than ownership positions in companies where he worked, he almost always only went long in investment grade bonds.

That careful nature obviously was the result of growing up during the Great Depression and World War II. My father had no safety net, no inheritance, no assistance, no stipends, no handouts, never received an allowance, and other than his mother rising early to prepare him breakfast in the early years of his professional career, he received little to no help from his family. His father gave him a last name and, perhaps, two or three good bits of wisdom. I mention this because as I read Dean Matt's fascinating dissection of the bourgeoning cannabis industry, I instantly recalled my father's oft-repeated "caravan" analogy. "Every five to ten years," my father told me many times, "a new caravan of assholes shows up on Wall Street with a new can't miss idea."

Those plaintive pleas from "the caravan" were roundly and summarily rejected. At times, my father recited the specifics of each of the periodic "can't miss" flare-ups. Based on his firsthand experience, he could trace the caravan's lineage of bubbles to the early 1950s. I neglected to jot down the specific examples of his caravan anecdote – one of my regrets now that my father is no longer alive – but from my firsthand experience I can recall the junk bond mania of the 1980s, the Dot.com mania of the 1990s, the mortgage backed security mania of the 2000s, the crypto currency mania of the 2010s, and now, as told from the perspective of an experienced financial executive, a new caravan has pulled into town touting yet another "can't miss" idea. Ladies and gentlemen, I give you the cannabis mania of the 2020s.

Lack of self-awareness is an attribute of the caravan and each time a new one flares up it has no idea that just a few years prior, a predecessor rolled through town and left in its wake a stream of losses, recrimination, lawsuits, and at times, indictments. The "can't miss" ideas may vary, but the caravan is the same. The players might be new, but their motivations, characteristics, traits, foibles, and predilections are the same as always. Naïve, wild eye, energetic, enigmatic, persuasive, and glib are their calling cards as they chase ephemeral riches and ill-defined profits from half-baked ideas, wrangle investment capital and board guidance from those who should know better, and extract labor and aspirational hopes from those who don't. Each caravan, therefore, is not new but merely the latest iteration of a bad idea.

The legalization of cannabis is perhaps long overdue. I personally have no interest in it nor is it a part of my life, but the classical liberal in me also believes society is better when the hand of government is light and individuals are left alone to freely make their own decisions about their lives. Despite myriad missteps and misrepresentations made by this most recent vintage of the caravan, many of which are succinctly and humorously laid out in this book you're about to read, the legalization – and commercialization – of cannabis will continue to gain in momentum. Genuine successes will happen. Fortunes will be made. And as with all manias, someone, somewhere, will crack the nut and create a sustainable business model, which in turn will be repeated and improved upon. Until then, Dean Matt's firsthand account of the early days of what he calls "Cannabis 2.0" should serve as a cautionary tale about what happens when the well intentioned, wild eyed naïfs of the caravan, as ill-prepared and sanguine as always, turn a new development into an age-old mania. We've seen this story before. And we'll see it again. The only question is will we learn?

-Bill Snow, author of *Mergers & Acquisitions For Dummies*

Preface

If you're like me, *and I know I am*, then you probably look forward to the carefree days of retirement, wondering what you'll be doing with a lot of time on your hands. A year ago, I was a fifty-something retired Chief Financial Officer (CFO) minding my own business, flying my plane, and traveling the country with my wife, usually with golf clubs in tow. As someone with more yesterdays than tomorrows, I valued fun, adventure, travel, relaxation, and living the dream.

Then the phone rang. A company needed a CFO.

Been there, done that. Usually, the conversation would have politely ended there. But this company was in the cannabis industry and had critical mass with dispensaries and cultivation facilities in several states and Puerto Rico. It also had a robust acquisition pipeline with opportunities in another half dozen or so states.

As Jake LaMotta said in *Raging Bull*: "*I heard some things.*"[1] In other words, I was curious, "Hmmm…. the cannabis industry." My interest was piqued. I was intrigued. The cannabis industry is unique because it is a mix of three established but very different sectors: cannabis is grown like an agricultural product, sold like a liquor product, and regulated like a pharmaceutical product.

As fate would have it, I was hired by this company in mid-2018 during the peak of the cannabis industry frenzy. Think, "Cannabis 2.0." (Cannabis 1.0 being the period from illegal weed up to the passage of full recreational use in Colorado and Washington.)

Fast forward just a few months to March 2019: After entertaining going public on our own, *we ended up selling our company for almost $1 billion* *in what was, at the time, the largest transaction in the history of the U.S. cannabis industry!*

Fast forward just nine more months to December 2019: cannabis industry stock prices have cratered and continue to be in free-fall. It's a shit show. *What just happened?*

Unless you were part of Holland's Tulip and Bulb Craze of the 1630s, the California Gold Rush in the mid-1800s, the Dot.com bubble around the turn of the century (i.e., to clarify for my smart-ass step-daughter, *2000* and not *1900*), the speculative housing bubble circa 2005-2008 or, most recently, the Bitcoin bubble in 2018, then perhaps you never experienced the challenges and opportunities presented by inefficient capital markets. In turbulent times, inefficient markets present arbitrage (i.e., money-making) opportunities, both on the way up, and the way down.

Investing, as with life in general, is all about figuring out if you are playing chess while others are playing checkers, or vice-versa. In the Summer of 2018, Cannabis 2.0 investors put cannabis entrepreneurs on a pedestal. These young entrepreneurs certainly appeared to be playing chess, maybe even the 3-dimensional kind. Some of the entrepreneurs convinced themselves, first, and then investors, second, that they were World Grandmasters, so billions poured into the industry.

But it turns out they were playing checkers all along.

As of 2020 Q1, cannabis company valuations are *50% - 75% less* than only the year prior. Cannabis industry participants and investors are trying to figure out, "Who is the fool in the room? Who will be stuck holding the bag when the music stops?" Often it's them, the face staring at them in the mirror.

The global *legal* cannabis industry is expected to triple in size from $9.5 billion in 2017 to $32 billion by 2022,[2] and as with any rapidly growing industry, fortunes will be made for sure. But when? Thus far, Cannabis 2.0 has turned out to be quite the pump fake. Almost across the board, company and industry projections have been too rosy and routinely missed. The markets don't take kindly to missed projections, and the cannabis industry is not immune to this basic tenet of the stock markets. As a result, cannabis company stock prices cratered. You know, *fool me once*. Investors continue to lick their wounds.

With all the carnage, is the cannabis industry circa 2020 Q1 a good investment? Do opportunities for *colossal* returns still exist? If so, are they worth the risk? Will investment in today's cannabis industry mint billionaires like the winners from other industries who live in Silicon Valley, Malibu, and New York City penthouses? They certainly didn't make their fortunes by being represented by a union, working a lot of overtime or getting paid double time on holidays. But don't forget to consider the investors in Enron, Bitcoin, WorldCom, Bernie Madoff Investment Securities, and other poster children of companies that litter the streets with broken dreams, having ruined millions of investors' golden years.

To clean up the cannabis industry's current mess, it needs experienced executives from other sectors, both at the management and Board of Directors level. Think, "Cannabis 3.0." With time, the sins of Cannabis 2.0 will be cleansed. Perhaps Cannabis 3.0 will emerge from the ashes of Cannabis 2.0 and be everything that Cannabis 2.0 has, thus far, failed to deliver: "the next big thing," a disruptive industry for sure, with promises to employ hundreds of thousands; an industry that would, no doubt, mint thousands of million-aires, generate billions of tax revenue, and relieve pain for millions of people.

The history of cannabis is no flash in the pan. The recorded use of cannabis as a medicine goes back nearly five thousand years. The U.S. govern-ment currently lists marijuana as a Schedule I narcotic, along with heroin and LSD. The groundswell of medical and recreational (i.e., adult) use legislation in the states over the last half-dozen years is giving the middle finger to the feds as state-level legislation conflicts with Uncle Sam's position on marijuana.

No doubt, most of these laws at the state level start with a limited scope for medicinal purposes (i.e., "medical marijuana") for a couple of dozen chronic ailments like lupus, multiple sclerosis, Parkinson's, rheuma-toid arthritis and more. But are the claims about the healing powers of the cannabis plant based on scientific research (i.e., *JAMA*[3]*-quality* scientific stud-ies), or, instead, just anecdotal, experiential "studies" from stoners and other marijuana industry folk heroes? Are the claims that the cannabis plant has miraculous healing properties just a smokescreen by industry pioneers and predatory governments with their eyes on the tax revenue prize? Or, is this really the beginning of total recreational use legalization across the United States and the world? Currently, most every state has some form of legalized marijuana laws on their books. Should the U.S. fund extensive studies by the U.S. Food and Drug Administration (FDA) to objectively determine the medicinal value and limitations of the cannabis plant?

Let's not be naïve: states are desperate to increase their revenues. Most states tread lightly into the controversial area of cannabis legalization by first enacting medical marijuana legislation and trying to disguise the ultimate objective: to generate as much tax revenue as possible. Quite a scheme: pull at the heartstrings of all state residents who most certainly know someone who has one of the couple dozen or so ailments for which the state will allow the medical use of marijuana. After all, who is going to object to a state that is so concerned about the welfare of its citizens? A state that wants to reduce the pain and suffering of its citizens? But don't succumb to this initial posturing because very few states have stopped at just medical use legislation. Most states have their eyes on the larger and more lucrative recreational use prize.

In most states where medical marijuana is the "loss leader," it only takes two or three more years before the states themselves are addicted . . . addicted to the tax revenue generated by this nascent medical marijuana industry. The states think, "Heck, if we can generate a lot of revenue from 1% of its residents that are in the medical marijuana system, imagine how much revenue we can generate if 25% or more of our residents buy marijuana products when we expand the program to adult or recreational use at higher tax rates!" The need for ever-increasing tax revenue is the crack cocaine that unites all the states (not some song about purple mountains majesty). Taxes from cannabis are rapidly becoming an increasingly popular revenue source that states count on to help support their runaway spending; most of our fifty states' department of revenues are becoming addicted to it. Unless or until fiscal responsibility becomes commonplace in state budgets, tax revenue afforded by legalizing cannabis is a *need* and not a *want*. In the U.S., states that have balanced budgets are the exception and not the rule. Most states will *need* the tax revenues from marijuana to help balance their budgets.

To maximize tax revenues generated from marijuana, some states are designing their adult-use programs to promote cannabis tourism. For instance, step off the plane at McCarran International in Las Vegas, and you're ten minutes away from the largest dispensary in the world, doing $5 million a month in revenue. In Nevada, a recreational use state, you are not required to be a resident of Nevada to purchase marijuana products. Consumption lounges (think marijuana bars), where you can partake of your cannabis purchase and relax with other like-minded folks, are the next big thing in Vegas and elsewhere. But, remember, you can't (legally) take it home with you because you currently can't cross state lines with marijuana products. "*What happens in Vegas stays in Vegas*" indeed!

We've all seen this movie before starring Sin City. I'm old enough to remember a time when you had to fly to Las Vegas if you wanted to gamble. Then, Atlantic City legalized gambling. After that came state lotteries, followed by multi-state lotteries. Soon, riverboat casinos were legalized, and state statutes required them to unmoor from the dock and float in a body of water before gambling could commence. Then, land-based casinos sprouted up on the sovereign land of almost every Indian nation. Shortly thereafter, the "*river*" requirement in *river*boat gambling was waived and folks could finally gamble on terra firma (without the risk of being seasick). Next, video poker and gaming in restaurants, bars, and the like was legalized. More recently, daily fantasy sports betting sites like *FanDuel* and *DraftKings* rolled out. Currently, sportsbook betting has expanded in multiple states.

Regardless of the vice, once their foot is in the door, the formula is the same for the states: start gingerly and don't upset the general population. Get them used to the new vice. Then open the door wide and rake in the tax revenues. Oh, by the way, just like the taxes on alcohol and smoking, the taxes on these vices (casinos, gambling, and now, cannabis) are, for the most part, regressive taxes that sometimes target and, most always, disproportionately and negatively impact the poorest of our citizens.

Let's look at the next vice to potentially be taxed, again with roots in Nevada: prostitution. Already states are dipping their toe in the water with many taxing legalized and regulated massage parlors. In all but the most conservative bible-belt regions of the U.S., it won't be long until full-fledged prostitution begins to spread its wings. Lawmakers justify the potential tax grab, "We might as well legalize it just like marijuana because it is happening in the black market anyway. By legalizing it, we will have a framework to keep sex-workers and customers safe, create jobs, and collect tax revenue." Blah, blah, blah.

As I write this book, the cannabis industry has evolved from the development of legal frameworks for newly legalized medical and recreational markets in 2016 to major "land grabs," the creation of the Multi-State Operators (MSOs), and the emergence of publicly-traded cannabis companies in 2018. Cannabis company valuations have never been higher than they were in early 2019; however, less than a year later, the industry (How do I put this?) *shit the bed*. In the second half of 2019, it's been like a circus, a shit show with cannabis industry company valuations in a freefall. It's amazing, really, how a small group of a few self-proclaimed cannabis visionaries has caused such financial harm to millions. Most cannabis industry stocks are trading near all-time lows as of 2020 Q1. The bloom is off the bud. This book helps to explain why and also explores the industry's prospects for the future.

Whatever your interest is in the cannabis industry — whether as an investor, employee, customer, bank, vendor, third-party consultant or other professional, regulator, business school professor, human resource manager, or a citizen wanting to learn more — buckle-up and ask yourself one thing: "Am I playing checkers or am I playing chess?" Time will tell . . . stay tuned!

A Few Notes

In determining a title for the book, it became evident to me that younger readers may never have heard the term "Gone to Pot." I took for granted that everyone has heard this expression just as it has been part of my vernacular growing up. My dad would always express concern with the direction the world was moving by saying, "This world is going to pot." Other Baby Boomers have, no doubt, also heard their parents commiserate that "the world is going to pot" at their dinner tables as well.

At the time, I thought that my dad was linking the degeneration of civility, respect for my elders and the like, to the increasing use of marijuana (i.e., pot) by the sixties and seventies counterculture groups like hippies. I assumed, like many, that the "gone to pot" idiom literally referred to marijuana.

But this is not the case. The genesis of the phrase "Gone to Pot" has its roots back to the 1500s, long before marijuana was prevalent among English speaking populations. One speculation is that the phrase's origin stemmed from the assertion that only the worst, toughest cuts of meat were thrown into a stew and cooked in a pot. In any event, "Gone to Pot" means "fallen into a horrible state,"[4] and that is where the cannabis industry finds itself as we enter 2020.

One unalienable truth about the cannabis industry is that it moves lightning fast. People talk about the cannabis industry in terms of *dog* years (i.e., seven years of growth and innovation in "normal industries" is crammed into just one year in the cannabis industry). Because of this dynamic, some of the facts and industry statistics I cite in the writing of this book may be out of date by the time it is published. As such, I apologize for any inaccuracies.

Additionally, because I live in Illinois, I am familiar with its cannabis laws and government more than those of other states. At times it may seem as if I am ridiculing Illinois, its governance, and problems. Full disclosure: I am. Why? Because it is arguably, the worst-run state in the history of our country and will continue to be as long as Illinois' citizens continue to elect corrupt, ineffective, and fiscally irresponsible miscreants into office year after year.

Once in a while, you may catch me going off-course with some personal rants, mostly about the state of politics. I was going to delete these rants, but my therapist suggested they are cathartic for me, and so they remain. If you are offended, please remember you have been warned. I offer no apologies.

Sprinkled in these pages, you'll come across (attempts at) humor (some better than others). That's just the inner stand-up comic in me trying to keep you engaged and turning these pages. (C'mon . . . lighten up. After all, it's only a book.) Feel free to laugh or heckle. (Either way, I won't hear you.)

I based this book on my personal experience and observations in the cannabis industry gleaned from my interactions with hundreds of other cannabis industry insiders in dozens of cannabis industry companies, including my capacity as a cannabis industry C-level executive and consultant. My opinions, commentary, and speculations are formed not only by my time spent in the cannabis industry itself but also, *and more importantly*, by my over thirty years' experience in a variety of commercial enterprises, from start-ups to *Fortune 100* companies . . . a perspective that very few thirty and forty-somethings in today's cannabis industry have.

That said, I do not consider myself an industry expert by any means, but, unlike many at the helms of Cannabis 2.0 companies, *I know what I don't know.* I don't claim that my observations are correct (How is "correct" defined anyway?) The thoughts in this book are just one part of the tapestry of perspectives that you should continue to gather so that you can form your own opinions about the industry. Talk to your broker, interview cannabis company CEOs, read *their* books, talk to your priest, or whomever. Every story has many sides. Go and find them.

Also, this book is not a debate on whether cannabis should or should not be legal. Other authors have written better books for that (I recommend *The Cannabis Manifesto* by Steve DeAngelo[5]).

This book is merely a collection of *dirty little secrets* about the cannabis industry that I believe those outside the industry would be shocked to hear of and more than interested in reading about. In this book, I tell stories from *Company A* through *Company Z* and more (I ran out of letters), which illustrate and expose these *dirty little secrets*. You'll hear these stories through my unique lens: a classically trained MBA and someone from outside the industry with a traditional business background, who quickly became an insider in the Wild West of the cannabis industry.

I present to you these stories and facts as I have personally observed and encountered them, from trusted sources, from the cannabis industry movers and shakers, and from publicly available documents. I have taken the liberty to change some of the identifying characteristics of industry individuals and companies such as names, locations, physical properties, and the like for privacy and other reasons. These changes won't influence the conclusions and impressions you will reach, you'll still get the picture.

My experience in the cannabis industry continues as I write this book and is a helluva roller coaster ride, complete with a colorful cast of characters, many of whom masquerade as seasoned business owners. Stories of fiduciary irresponsibility and greed are plentiful. Not surprisingly, you will find similar stories with only minor variations across multiple companies in the industry. I've collected some of the most incredulous ones herein to both inform and warn those looking to break into or invest in the cannabis industry. I had to leave many other stories on the cutting room floor.

Lest you think that the cannabis industry monopolizes the absurd, I've included an *Intermission* between each *Dirty Little Secret* chapter for your amusement and entertainment. These additional "shake your head and roll your eyes" wild and ridiculous stories will help you to draw parallels from other industries and from different times to the cannabis industry of today.

So, sit back and buckle up while I take you on quite the ride through the cannabis industry as you read the incredulous, intriguing, and fascinating contents of this book. Welcome to the shit show.

Dean K. Matt
Spring, 2020

INTRODUCTION

RETIREMENT INTERRUPTED

It was the best of nines; it was the worst of nines. I always wanted to write a book and start like this. Drop mic? Not quite. Read on.

I love a good round of golf. I carded a six-over-par for a forty-two on the front nine, on pace for a respectable (at least for me) round in the eighties. But I blew up on the back nine and once again shot in the 100s. (I'm sure many of you can relate.) To put it bluntly: I played bad, really bad. So bad, that *the best two balls I hit all day was when I stepped on the rake in the sand trap!*

Such was our round at our local course in suburban Chicago on a rather typical, humid day in July 2018. My playing partner was my wife, who took up the sport only five years prior and has been my best bud on and off the course for some time now.

Having recently retired from the rat race of the financial world, my wife and I had a life that included vast doses of travel and golf. A pilot since high school and an aircraft owner since the '90s (again, for the benefit of my smart-ass step-daughter, that's the *1990s* and not the *1890s*), I schlepped my wife all over the country in our four-passenger Cessna 172SP, spending our free time traveling and golfing. Earlier that year, we stretched our legs and tested our Cessna's range (and our patience as a married couple in the cramped quarters of a single-engine general aviation aircraft) on a golf and sightseeing adventure to Sedona and Scottsdale . . . but I digress.

THE PHONE CALL

Content with my first six months of retirement at the age of fifty-eight (and figuring I have about twelve more "good" years of flying and golf before the aches and pains of old age would curtail our lifestyle), I received a phone call: a *cannabis company had an immediate opening for a Chief Financial Officer*. I wasn't even looking in earnest for employment anymore but was still receiving plenty of phone calls from companies and recruiters, and junk e-mails from the job search robots from which I was just too lazy to unsubscribe.

This opportunity piqued my interest. I heard a lot about the cannabis industry but did not know much about it, apart from some personal research I performed while attending the University of Illinois in the early '80s (again, for clarity, the *1980s*). I thought, "Hmmm . . . certainly worth checking out and beginning a dialogue." I was indifferent as to whether I wanted to return to the workforce and interrupt my new carefree lifestyle of no worries and no stress. I call the shots.

Little did I know the adventure that lay ahead. So, I quickly updated and fired off my standard resume, *without* customizing it for this particular job opening (in violation of advice from just about every job search expert who always stress taking the time to customize your resume to the job specifications).

In any event, I quickly forgot about my conversation with the company and submission for this opportunity. My wife and I hit the golf links a few more times over the next few weeks. So, I was a bit surprised when, a few weeks later, I received another phone call from the cannabis company indicating interest in meeting with me.

The interview

I would meet with the founders one Summer afternoon at their brand-new office space. At my age, I didn't feel like dressing up for an interview anymore. (After all, it is a marijuana company. How formal can it be?) Violating the interview rule that stresses you should err on the side of over-dressing rather than under-dressing, I put on jeans and a shirt. (I couldn't even tell you if I tucked it in or not.) I guess my "*I don't give a shit factor*" has increased over the years. I realized that this was the age I was becoming my father!

I drove to a trendy section of Chicago where this pot company was located. This area was known more for restaurants and entertainment venues than for office space. That said, for some reason, about a half-dozen marijuana companies called this area of Chicago home.

I hate going to the big city where the parking and the traffic are not for me. Give me the suburbs any day. Would I really want to come out of retirement for a job that has a sixty-mile round-trip commute consuming over two precious hours each day, the equivalent of nine holes of golf?

As I sat awaiting my interview in the storefront office, I mentally mulled over some questions and topics of conversation: "What happened to the previous CFO? Tell me about the company's culture. How is the company funded? Is the company cash flow positive? If not, what is the monthly cash burn? Is a stock compensation plan in place? How much capital and debt does the company have?"

In today's world, it is also probably prudent to see the company's employee handbook regarding their Sexual Harassment Policy or Google the owners' police records. But I thought these topics might cross a line when meeting with a company for the first time.

As I waited, I surveyed the landscape: only two offices that I could see, including one with glass walls (a.k.a. the "fishbowl"), about ten desks, and no conference rooms . . . nothing that anyone who had ever worked in an office environment would find functional at all. As I continued to wait, I sat and sized up the office. I had a lot of additional questions running around in my head: "Where do people meet? Where do human resources personnel hold confidential discussions?" (Call me old-fashioned, but do all employees need to know about Betty's upcoming goiter surgery?) "Where would I, as CFO, store all of the company's confidential and sensitive financial documents?" And, "Why a storefront retail space on a busy street?" After all, the company was not permitted to sell cannabis out of this location, so why does it need to be located in a retail storefront? Probably no thought process other than it could be a ten-minute walk from one of the owner's apartments. Or, so that all the incoming traffic to Chicago would drive by this office and see the company's name as they got off of the highway.

As I would later find out, one of the founders, Greg, was all about shiny objects and glitz. I would have gone 180 degrees in the opposite direction — find a functional but nondescript office that flies under the radar. Why draw all of this unnecessary attention to a marginally legal company? Especially in this industry.

My priorities regarding office space functionality and location were apparently irrelevant to the founders, as they must not have encountered them in their previous collective experience: Greg as an ambulance-chasing attorney, and Hal as a small business owner. Having never worked in a corporate environment, Greg was clueless as to the bare necessities needed in an office that would allow the company to achieve the scale he dreamed of when visions of sugarplums danced in his head. Features like conference rooms, private offices, and other basics of office functionality were not on Greg's radar screen when he went shopping for this office space.

Also, while I didn't see any, I assumed the office had bathrooms with functioning toilets, not because the founders thought of them, but only because the great City of Chicago's Department of Code Enforcement would most likely require them. To deviate from code would, of course, require a customary kickback as seemingly everyone in the Chicago government has their hand out. You know, "*no ticky, no washy.*"

In summary, my first impression was that the place was a dump and not conducive to the efficient functioning of building a business that was preparing to go public on the Toronto Stock Exchange (my observation would later turn out to be spot on). While it was a trendy, "loft-like" space — the kind the kids think is cool — it was dysfunctional from an operating perspective. The office had no conference rooms, no privacy, no printers, and only about four telephones in the entire office. It makes it hard to transfer calls to someone without a phone. I guess they handle most calls through individuals' cell phones. I would later learn that they conduct conference calls with up to a dozen employees gathered around a cell phone turned on speaker mode. But, of course, how would these founders know anything about the basics of a functioning office? *They never worked for anyone before.*

Meet Hal, a late thirty-something entrepreneur who is a real workhorse. His previous success was building a chain of, effectively, high-end donut shops. Through these shops Hal was reeling in the dough — definitely helpful in the marijuana industry where you'll need about $200 thousand to complete a winning license application; and should you win a license, you'll need lots o' cash to fund the $10 - $15 million to begin building out a cultivation facility or the $250 thousand to $1 million to open a dispensary. It's not like you can stroll into your neighborhood bank with 10% equity and a business plan and walk out with a loan for the 90% you don't have. That's because the traditional banking system that we all take for granted is off-limits when it comes to the cannabis industry. There are no loans, no checking accounts, and no credit cards, but more on this later.

Hal is an engaging person who can spin a story with the best of them. While his hands-on management style has made him successful in the food-service industry, the question that remains for many budding entrepreneurs like Hal entering the cannabis industry is, "does your life experiences and talents in one industry translate to success in the cannabis industry?" I give a lot of entrepreneurs I've encountered over the years a definite "A" for effort, but the simple truth is that it is the rare few who can take their businesses to the proverbial "next level." The reasons for potential failure in the cannabis industry are many:

- Lack of cannabis experience (you need to learn on the fly);

- Lack of being able to swim with the sharks and navigate through the greed that permeates the industry (unless you're a *great white* yourself);
- Lack of understanding that operating in a regulated industry with many shareholders requires a level of transparency and candor that entrepreneurs have not experienced in the running of their previous, privately-held businesses;
- Inability to delegate (you can't scale a company if you're still making all the decisions and signing all the checks);
- Lack of understanding or prioritization for the need to build out back-office functions like human resources and finance to support growth;
- Lack of experience in the unique dynamic of a geographically decentralized organization with over 200 employees vs. experience in business with just a handful of employees and a cash register;
- Lack of understanding that the third-party professionals (i.e., tax, legal, and insurance professionals, etc.) which small-business entrepreneurs have relied on, and are usually comprised of friends and family, more often than not lack the level of experience, intellect, and sophistication needed when dealing with the issues faced by larger companies;
- and more!

Hal was Russian, and his *go-to* guys in operations, legal, and other areas were mostly Russian as well. They shared Hal's tireless work ethic. Hal's "Russian mafia" was frugal, resourceful, and street smart. They "figured it out" whenever they encountered a potential show-stopper. They were not book smart or elegant in their solutions, but they got it done, albeit with a ton of chaos, inefficiency, and missteps. Such is the level of professionalism and operational infrastructure at most Cannabis 2.0 companies.

This combination of street-smarts, grit, and almost singular focus on looking out for #1, mostly at the expense of others, undoubtedly led to Hal's success with his donut shop empire and would serve Hal well in his quest toward an eight or nine-figure payday in the cannabis industry.

Hal's partner Greg was also scrappy and competitive. He lacked financial capital, but likewise, he had a good feel for the emerging cannabis business. Before teaming up with Hal around 2015, for a short time, Greg practiced personal injury law in the ambulance-chasing end of the legal spectrum — the kind that advertises on daytime television during *Jerry Springer*. Like Hal, Greg was intrigued by the cannabis industry and began applying for licenses in various states. Greg had a true entrepreneurial spirit and read the early cannabis industry tea leaves correctly: these licenses would be worth a lot of money someday — and sooner than anyone thought. While Greg prided himself on his deal-making ability, I wasn't too impressed. He relied on his gut and emotions and lacked the objectivity crucial to building a sustainable business. He had no previous business experience in acquisitions and negotiating deals. When the veneer was peeled back, there didn't seem to be much in the way of Mergers and Acquisitions (M&A) financial horsepower.

After a few years of cobbling some companies together, Hal and Greg found themselves in the right place at the right time, the cannabis industry of 2018. The stars have aligned for these two. Many successful entrepreneurs were hard-working, and some were lucky. Hal and Greg were both.

After exchanging pleasantries in the open office, the interview morphed over into the fishbowl. I was indifferent and not really giving it my best effort. If I got the job, great; if not, like baseball and hockey players who lost their last playoff game and cleaned out their lockers, I'd head back to the golf course.

Hal and Greg stood up as they interviewed me, partly because they couldn't sit still but mainly because the office did not have enough chairs. It was clear that these were not polished Fortune 500 executives. They weren't the Wall Street caliber executives who I've worked with in the past. On many levels, this was amateur hour; but amateur hour was just fine with me as I've also been involved with many family and privately held companies before. With cannabis emerging as the Dot.com event of their lifetime, they had a potentially huge growth trajectory. While they were sitting on a potential goldmine, I wondered more than once if they had the strategy and skills to unearth, mine, and monetize that gold.

If I was given bad marks from traditional executive recruiters on how to prepare for and act during an interview, then the founders were given horrible marks on how to conduct one. But this wasn't a traditional industry, so all bets were off and all formalities out the window. Internet job sites (like LinkedIn, Monster, Indeed, and the like) are full of advice on how to properly conduct oneself during an interview: how to sit and make eye contact, the proper time to send a thank you, etc. Cannabis 2.0 had no time for formalities, and I was too old to care. Instead, like the Dot.com era in the past, cannabis companies need to get their butts in seats and put it in drive . . . fast! Speed, not etiquette, or historical job search formulas is what matters from both the candidate's and the company's perspective in the cannabis industry. Showing up and being yourself is 90% of the key to success in getting a cannabis industry job. That continues to be the case today as each Multi-State Operator (MSO) cannabis company's website has hundreds of unfulfilled jobs that need filling pronto. No time to waste, no time for formalities. Get in there and take your best shot.

During the "interview," the founders were frequently distracted, fielding phone calls and texts throughout our talk. Neither Greg or Hal had ever worked with a CFO previously. As such, they did not understand the role of a CFO or of an accounting/finance department for that matter. To them, these functions were just a necessary evil to the really sexy part of the business, which was growing and selling weed along with "doing deals." But, doing deals requires a certain amount of financial acumen. They didn't realize this. They didn't have this arrow in their quivers. As I would later learn, to them, a CFO was just a glorified bookkeeper . . . not an integral part of the management team, not part of the inner circle, and certainly, not part of the Russian mafia. The only reason they thought they needed a CFO was that their investors knew an experienced, credible CFO would be required if they were going to take the company public.

After about thirty minutes, the "interview" was over. They said they were conducting about five interviews for the position, and "they'd let me know." I left and headed back to the golf course in search of a few birdies (and some balls I'd lost in previous rounds).

To my surprise, a few days later, I received an e-mail expressing interest in making me an offer to be their CFO. Not sure what they saw in me other than having certain elements in my experience that I knew provided immediate confidence to investors and instant credibility to the Leadership Team section of their pitch decks and website. I checked a lot of boxes: CFO, M&A, and Chief Operating Officer (COO) experience; start-up and Initial Public Offering (IPO) experience; the right mix of corporate/publicly-held Fortune 100 and acquisitive, privately-held company experience in a variety of industries. I looked great on paper — with an MBA in Finance from The University of Chicago (the #1 Business School for Finance the year I graduated) as well as a BS in Accountancy from the perpetual #1 accounting undergraduate program in the country — The University of Illinois. I would be the only person on the executive team with extensive, relevant experience in publicly-held companies. It also didn't hurt that I was immediately available . . . like the next week.

Having taken a company public before, I knew this was going to be a fixer-upper with a lot of work to do to make up for years of back-office neglect. But this wasn't anything new for me. In a position like this with a company at this size and stage of growth, I would expect a below-market salary component in exchange for the opportunity to participate in a yet-to-be-determined stock compensation/equity plan. In my discussions with Hal and Greg, I was candid in that I enjoyed retirement but would come off the bench if this opportunity could reasonably yield a total compensation package (fueled mostly by stock options, of course) of $5 million over the next two years. They walked me through the math and sensitivity analysis as they saw it and convinced me that I could reasonably expect a $5 million payday. And so, my excellent adventure began the next week, leaving me just enough time to squeeze in a quick golf trip to Iowa with my wife.

Long story short, this fifty-something (in a twenty to forty-something world) got the job that he was indifferent about getting. They didn't even ask for or check references! I could have majored in embezzlement with a minor in securities fraud for all they knew. So much for doing four rounds of interviews and completing those stupid Myers-Briggs Type Indicator personality fit tests! (All bullshit in my humble opinion anyway.)

I was now CFO of a $30+ million MSO in the cannabis industry — a company with operations in about a half dozen states plus Puerto Rico and untold non-operational licenses and license applications in another half-dozen states. The company was valued at about $75 million, consistent with the market values of similar companies in the cannabis industry at the time. Little did I (or anyone in the industry) know at that time that in just eight short months, the company's valuation would balloon to almost $1 *billion*, an astronomical (and unsustainable) valuation equal to 25-30x annual revenues. Compare this to the companies in your stock portfolio, and you'll say, "*I gots to get me some of that!*"

SOME INDUSTRY BACKGROUND

In 2018 Q3, the sexy, sweet-spot in the cannabis industry was these MSOs. More than just a mom-and-pop, onesie-twosie dispensary, these MSOs were vertically integrated and offered investors a critical mass of revenue, infrastructure, and a sizeable geographic presence with a footprint across several states. MSOs would be the *consolidators* and not the *consolidated*. Additionally, they were vertically integrated with cultivation facilities feeding their manufacturing or processing divisions which, in turn, fed their dispensaries. MSOs held several types of state-regulated licenses, including licenses for cultivation (i.e., cannabis growing facilities), retail (i.e., dispensaries which sell various cannabis products to customers), manufacturing (for the production of edibles and topicals and other cannabis-derived products), and in some states, distribution. With these licenses, a vertically integrated MSO will grow and harvest the marijuana and produce not only the combustibles (raw "flower," and pre-rolled joints), but also any number of extracted and manufactured products such as edibles (gummies, tinctures, shatter, chocolates, brownies, and other baked goods) and topicals (sprays and oils).

MSOs were highly valued because they made for a great story to be told by investment bankers chomping at the bit to take them public, albeit on the Canadian exchanges. The opportunity to be an early stage-investor in a privately-held MSO that was preparing to go public was very attractive to many investors. Investors were more than eager to invest at an early stage in these companies and reap the benefits associated with the increased valuations when these companies went public. Raising money in the cannabis industry in 2018 Q3 was not difficult and more than a couple dozen high-profile cannabis companies had either gone public or were gearing up to go public. In the cannabis industry of 2018 Q3, raising money was a lay-up, not a three-point shot from half court.

When you think of "going public," you may think Initial Public Offering (IPO). In the world of cannabis, however, companies that are so called "plant-touching" (meaning they grow, produce, manufacture, and/or distribute marijuana) cannot go public on the U.S. regulated stock exchanges as they are not compliant with federal law. Remember, growing, distributing, and selling marijuana is illegal at the federal level.

In the U.S., marijuana is still a "Schedule I" narcotic, making it federally illegal. In the eyes of Uncle Sam, marijuana is as dangerous as other Schedule I drugs like LSD or heroin, and apparently, more dangerous than Schedule II drugs like cocaine and methamphetamine. Many pro-cannabis groups think it is ridiculous that marijuana is still listed as a Schedule I narcotic despite the (debatable) folklore that no one has ever died from overdosing on it.

So, these MSOs are typically taken public on the Canadian exchanges like the Canadian Stock Exchange (CSE), or Toronto Stock Exchange (TSX) which were receptive to registering the shares of plant-touching cannabis companies. Companies like Canopy Growth Corporation, Green Thumb Industries, Aurora Cannabis, Tilray, and others garnered big headlines and even bigger valuations as publicly-traded companies in mid-2018. Most of the companies going public on the Canadian exchanges do so in what is called a Reverse Take Over (RTO) in which a U.S.-based company buys one of the many dormant (i.e., "shell") companies on one of the Canadian exchanges. Then, in a labyrinth of legal entity manipulation engineered by $800 per hour corporate and tax attorneys, the U.S.-based company effectively merges into the Canadian shell and its shares become publicly-traded.

While the Canadian stock exchanges are less liquid and not as preferred as their U.S. counterparts (i.e., NASDAQ or NYSE), U.S. investors can easily invest in these Canadian listed stocks via the OTCQX market which is a market for companies already listed on a qualified international stock exchange. It is generally believed that when (*not if*) the U.S. government no longer lists marijuana as a Schedule I narcotic and when (*not if*) cannabis companies begin trading on the U.S. exchanges, that cannabis company valuations will be higher than similar companies listed on the Canadian exchanges, reflecting the more extensive visibility that the NYSE and NASDAQ exchanges offer, leading to better volumes and liquidity.

In November 2019, the U.S. House Judiciary Committee passed the Marijuana Opportunity Reinvestment and Expungement (MORE) Act. The MORE Act would remove marijuana from Schedule I of the Controlled Substances Act. Not surprisingly, the cannabis stocks reacted positively to this news for a few days (mostly because the industry did not have much good news at the time). Forward progress like this is expected along the path toward federal legalization, but full federal legalization is still years away and this measure is not likely to make it to the full House for consideration until later in 2020, at the earliest. (You may have noticed that the House and Senate have been a bit preoccupied of late.) Even if the MORE Act passes in the House, it is expected to be voted down in the Republican-controlled Senate.

Taking a company public in Canada includes many untold costs, including but not limited to U.S. and Canadian auditors, securities, and corporate counsel, underwriting fees, and exchange listing fees. The one-time direct cost for Cannabis 2.0 companies preparing for an RTO (including Directors and Officers insurance and third party legal, accounting, tax, and audit professionals) is in the $2 - $3 million range. For a time in 2018 Q4, it was rumored that Canadian citizens who were investors or professionals servicing the many U.S. cannabis companies who also intended to travel to the U.S., regardless of business or pleasure, would not be allowed entry into the U.S. by U.S. Immigration and Customs Enforcement. Many Canadian investors did not want to take the chance of being flagged at the border and forever barred from entering the U.S., so many Canadian investors insisted that any meetings related to their U.S. cannabis investments take place north of the border in Canada as opposed to stateside. Other Canadian cannabis investors were reluctant to continue to do deals with U.S. companies at all.

An often-overlooked category of "cost" is the *time* necessary to get these cannabis companies to the market. Seeing the success of several cannabis industry RTOs that occurred in the Summer of 2018, a number of U.S. cannabis companies came out of the woodwork and planned to go public as well. It was their *me-too* moment. The problem is that you can't just wake up as a private company in July and decide you want to be a public company by August. Nor can you decide in Q3 that you want to go public in Q4. It doesn't happen that way. Going public requires a "been there done that" management team, audits, systems, internal controls credibility, and integrity. Just about every function or aspect of a privately-run business needs to be upgraded and improved, sometimes even replacing its CEO, the founders, and other C-suite executives. The time it takes to prepare a company to transition from a private to a public company is at least six-months in the best of conditions, but, realistically, closer to a year.

Many cannabis MSO owners' and investors' naïveté were on full display in the Summer of 2018 by seriously believing that their company could transform from a private company to a public company within just a few months. Based on my own IPO experience, echoed by just about every reputable auditor and legal counsel servicing Cannabis 2.0, taking a private company public in just a few months was nothing but delusional, wishful thinking. Someone had to tell the emperor that he had no clothes. I stepped up to add that role to my resume many times in the past.

With the cannabis market ripe and thirsting for additional RTOs in September 2018, cannabis companies and their investors were looking to shortcut the process and take their companies public even though they weren't ready. The thought process for these large investors was to score big while the market was red hot, then cash out and move on, leaving retail investors holding the bag. Capitalize on the hype, the bubble. Pump and dump. (***Author's note:*** To a large extent, that is what happened.) Yep . . . the emperor had no clothes, indeed!

HAL AND GREG'S EXCELLENT ADVENTURE

Immediately after winning one of the first cultivation licenses in Illinois, Hal and the Russian mafia moved to the middle of nowhere, Illinois, to build a cultivation center. Knowing nothing about growing marijuana, knowing nothing of designing and building a cultivation center, they got to work and figured it out along the way. In these tasks, Hal was in his element, and no one was better, more resourceful, or more driven. He had a take-no-prisoners mindset. Within a year, Hal opened one of the first licensed cultivation centers in Illinois, a medical marijuana state (requiring a doctor's prescription for a couple of dozen or so listed ailments and a state issued medical marijuana card that the state uses for tracking patients' purchases somewhere in the bowels of its computer systems).

Before long, Hal's company harvested its first marijuana crop and began shipping to the dispensaries opening up across the state. The process was simple and lacked sophistication. The cultivation center salesperson would advise the dispensaries what products were available for shipping the next week, and the dispensaries would place orders. The product offerings changed weekly and were highly dependent on the marijuana supply at the cultivation center.

Products included traditional buds, pre-rolled joints, products infused with THC (the part of the cannabis plant that would get you high), and CBD products (which do not get you high but claim to have certain medicinal and healing effects). Other products included gummies or baked goods (insert your college or high school "marijuana brownie" image here), shatter, tinctures, infused beverages, and more.

In the cannabis industry, the growers need the dispensaries, and the dispensaries need the growers; thus, holders of these licenses formed many interdependent relationships. The cannabis industry is notorious for joint ventures. With all the interconnections of various and myriad legal entities, the legal ownership charts look like spaghetti thrown against the wall.

Hal's growth path was no exception. As he met others in the industry, they would join forces in a maze of tangled ownership for various legal, tax, and control reasons. So, Hal met Greg and then another person named Steve, who had some licenses in other states. Together, they formed a new company which made investments in Nevada which, unlike Illinois at the time, was a recreational marijuana state as of January 1, 2017. Soon after, Hal and Greg made additional investments on the East Coast as well.

By 2017 and 2018, it became increasingly evident that the cannabis industry was ripe for consolidation. Investors would pump billions of dollars into MSOs to enable them to gobble up smaller dispensaries and grow centers, and add them to their ever-expanding networks.

SSDI: Same Shit, Different Industry

I've seen this industry consolidation story before. My first job out of college was as a Division Controller for Waste Management circa the mid-eighties. At the time, Waste Management was a very well-run company. Its auditors were the best in the business: Arthur Andersen. Who would have "thunk" that in less than twenty years, both Arthur Andersen and Waste Management would both be out of business due to scandal?

Today's Waste Management has its genesis as USA Waste,
which picked up the carcass of the *original* Waste Management
assets when it went out of business.

H. Wayne Huizenga, a truly world-class entrepreneur, led the *original* Waste Management. Wayne's nephew worked for me on a project in the corporate offices in Oak Brook, IL. He came to me one day with his tanned skin, neatly pressed suit, Polo tie and cologne (both fashionable back in the day), and ever-present smile (Wouldn't you smile if your uncle was Wayne Huizenga?) and said, "Hey Dean, my uncle is working on something. Take a look at this." He handed me a marketing brochure. I reviewed it and, after a minute or so, inquired, "What the hell is a *Blockbuster Video*?" I never heard of such a thing. Wayne's nephew went on to explain that his uncle was leaving Waste Management for the next big thing: video rental. I was fascinated, it was the 1980s and "high tech" VCRs (the kind that blinked "12:00" and your grandparents asked you to set up for them) were just beginning to penetrate households across the U.S.

Before Blockbuster, consumers rented videos from mom-and-pop video rental stores that had sprung up all over. In case you're too young to remember, in addition to the main video rental floor, these stores usually had an "adult section," generally behind curtains or a door, where shoppers could find X-rated videos (and creepy old men). Blockbuster was well capitalized and positioned to consolidate the mom-and-pop video rental industry. It had a world-class management team that had already proven its disciplined approach in acquiring companies in a consolidating industry, which, in turn, led to an unlimited supply of money from Wall Street to execute its plan. After a few years of exponential store growth, Wayne and his "Dutch mafia" investors, who already had made billions on Waste Management, took Blockbuster public in the late 1980s. They had the Midas touch, the secret-sauce.

American culture would forever be transformed with families visiting these Blockbuster stores all over the U.S. to rent movies (at the time, there was no such thing as the internet, video-on-demand, or streaming services).

At its peak, Blockbuster had over 9,000 stores, 84,000 employees, and 43 million card carrying members worldwide.

Wayne had a knack for building and scaling companies in industries ripe for consolidation. More importantly, Wayne knew when to sell what he built, exiting these businesses at their peak valuations, leaving someone else to hold the bag. Soon, Wayne saw storm clouds on the horizon for the video rental industry from new, emerging entertainment content delivery methods like video-on-demand and new companies with disruptive technologies like Netflix and Redbox. As such, he sought to sell Blockbuster. In 1994, media giant Viacom purchased Blockbuster in a deal valued at $8.4 billion. I guess the digit-heads at Viacom overpaid a wee bit too much for Blockbuster because just three years later, Viacom wrote down the value of the Blockbuster assets to $4.6 billion, resulting in an almost 50% loss in shareholder value.

> Blockbuster had also missed a big opportunity: they had a chance to purchase the then fledgling Netflix for $50 *million* in 2000. As of 2020 Q1, the value of Netflix is in the $150 *billion* range. *Missed it by that much.* Today, only one Blockbuster store remains, located in Bend, Oregon.

The point is that nothing lasts forever. Wayne Huizenga sold Blockbuster for $8.4 billion to Viacom, which, in turn, sold it for only $320 million to Dish Network. Ouch! Dish held onto Blockbuster until it wound down operations between 2013 and 2014. (***Author's note:*** I've seen too many business development folks get excited about making acquisitions at any price. In my view, some of the best "acquisitions" are the ones that aren't pursued at all.)

Wayne was also a significant investor and Chairman of many other "brand name" public companies like Republic Waste, Extended Stay America, Auto Nation USA, Boston Market, and more. At one time or another, he owned the Miami Dolphins, Joe Robbie Stadium, the Florida Marlins, and the Florida Panthers. Wayne was a genius at buying low and selling high. Maybe the garbageman in him made him keenly aware that one man's trash is another man's treasure? I can only imagine that at a young age, he was an expert at playing musical chairs, making sure he always had a nice seat when the music stopped. Wayne, a genuinely world-class entrepreneur, passed away in 2018, most certainly increasing the smile on his nephew's face.

In the cannabis industry thus far, I haven't seen anything close to the likes of a Wayne Huizenga emerge, even though most of the CEOs running today's cannabis companies fancy themselves as world-class entrepreneurs. I'm not impressed.

It reminds me of the 1988 vice-presidential debates when VP candidate Lloyd Bentsen famously put Dan Quayle in his place when he said, "Senator, I served with Jack Kennedy. I knew Jack Kennedy. Jack Kennedy was a friend of mine. Senator, you're no Jack Kennedy."[6]

I'd say the same to most of the current cannabis industry CEOs in comparing them to Wayne Huizenga.

BACK TO WORK — THE ADVENTURE BEGINS

After a seventy-five-minute drive to the Big City (it would have taken longer had I not left before daybreak to avoid the rush hour), I arrived in the parking lot, a convenient twenty-five step walk to the front door, at 7 am on a Thursday. (I usually don't like to start new jobs on Monday, too much of a transition from being idle to being thrown into the fire.) Working two days and then having the weekend off seems to work for me. Little did I know that weekend would be the last two days off I would have for the next eight months.

Mike, the company's Chief Legal Officer, met me upon my arrival. Like start-up companies from the Dot.com era and like every other cannabis company trying to go public, we had a lot of Chief X Officers. I guess it makes people feel important. Mike was likeable and similar to most of the folks that worked here, he worked long hours, in part to avoid morning and evening rush hours, but mostly because there was a shitload of work to do. This was not your typical 9 to 5 gig. His commute was as wicked as mine. Also, if we were successful, Mike wouldn't have to work another day in his life. Not bad for a thirty-something. That was the plan anyway.

Mike and I were the early birds. Most of the others strolled in, seemingly, when the sun woke them up. There was Jim in biz-development, Denise in customer service, Jennifer in sales, Arlene in packaging and graphics, Sue in administration, and more. Soon all ten desks were occupied, begging the question: "Where would additional head counts sit in this dysfunctional office set up?"

The office was usually chaotic, with no place for privacy or to meet with visitors. It was noisy and hard to hear yourself think. There was a basement that was large and open, and sometimes we'd hold meetings down there. The fishbowl had two desks in it, but there were often as many as eight people in there. At times it got so hot in the fishbowl that I thought I'd catch malaria. Chaos permeated both floors of the office. Confidential basement meetings were interrupted with employees walking (and occasionally running) to and from the bathrooms. On one occasion, knowing of an important meeting scheduled for the next day and seeing we were out of "provisions" in the bathrooms, I took it upon myself to bring a twelve-pack of toilet paper from home for the meeting. My wife thought I was nuts. I said, "Don't ask." This was a BYOTP type of company.

With so much to do, the hours flew by. There was a TV mounted to the wall typically tuned into the morning news, and before long, we'd hear "*You ARE the father*," indicating that *Maury* was on and it was 1 pm. Jennifer, in sales, sat closest to the television. I don't know how she sold anything over the phone with all the paternity test results blaring from the TV.

I quickly learned that our first order of business was to complete our "roll-up." As it currently stood, the company was a patchwork of various operating companies in many legal entities with a nucleus of common ownership. The roll-up is a legal process to consolidate ownership into a single Holding Company (HoldCo or the Mothership). Members, or shareholders, of these various, disparate companies will contribute their shares in "Dispensary A" (for example) in exchange for "Mothership HoldCo" shares. The process is not easy because a valuation methodology needs to be developed and applied to all the various companies being rolled-up. Of course, the owners of these companies tend to think that their company is worth more than the pre-scribed formulaic valuation and so the process is like herding cats.

Helpful to our process, however, were several valuation datapoints from recent and highly visible roll-ups, which became publicly-held companies on either the Toronto or Canadian Stock Exchange. Viewed as successful models and templates (at least *at that time,* but the world has changed in just a year) for our roll-up were Multi-State Operators such as Green Thumb Industries in Chicago, Canopy Growth Corporation in Toronto, Aurora Cannabis, and many others.

We had three dispensaries, three grow centers, and a joint- venture in a dispensary that we shared with a publicly-traded cannabis company that happened to have offices a few blocks away. The company had about forty different legal entities shaped by various legal, risk, and tax considerations. Many of these were holding companies (with no operating activities) or spe-cial purpose real estate companies that owned the property that the various operating companies utilized. Of course, in a company run by lawyers, the structure was overly complicated. The accountants reading this will appreci-ate that lawyers who put together various agreements, commission structures, contractual management fee agreements, etc. do so without any regard to how they needed to be accounted for. It's as if they say, "Wow, I crafted an elegant agreement with the other party. Here's the 200-page agreement for the accountants to read through to determine any accounting implications. Good luck!"

But it was still a patchwork of disparate companies. To drive further value, Hal needed to roll these companies up into one legal entity under one umbrella and build a credible management team. If these companies could be successfully rolled-up and an experienced management team assembled to run the show, this MSO's valuation would double. The valuation would roughly double again if the company went public. Along the way, incremen-tal acquisitions would further increase the company's valuation. Once rolled up under one legal entity, Hal's group of companies would be in the top dozen or so largest marijuana conglomerates in the country.

In the Fall of 2018, publicly-held cannabis companies were being valued at least in the twenty-times revenue range. Let me repeat that. The twenty-times revenue range meant that if your marijuana company has $20 million in revenue, then it is valued at $400 million. By contrast, let's say you had a company in the mature food industry where your $20 million revenue company is worth about *one-half* times its annual revenues, or $10 million. You do the math. Where would you rather be?

The valuations in the mature world of food processing seem rather boring when compared with Cannabis 2.0 companies. In October 2018, there was an announcement of a particularly high-profile cannabis industry transaction. MedMen announced the purchase of PharmaCann for $682 million, implying absurd multiples. My calculator doesn't go that high. Of course, valuations also reflect risk. With food processing, your returns arc relatively predictable and safe when compared to, say, the often-volatile technology sector or burgeoning new industries like cannabis.

Keep in mind that in cannabis, for instance, there can be no assurance that the federal government doesn't wake up one day and enforce federal law, which would, effectively, shut down the entire industry. Investors require higher valuation multiples commensurate with this increased risk. After all, billions of invested dollars could become all but worthless overnight with the stroke of someone's pen in our nation's capital.

By comparison, in the food industry, it is doubtful that Uncle Sam would ever tell you to "*Let go of your Eggo!*" and thus, investment risk in the relatively mature food processing industry is much less than in the cannabis industry.

The risk of the U.S. government enforcing federal law and shutting down the cannabis industry is undoubtedly a risk, albeit generally thought to be a risk with a low probability of occurring. Other risks undertaken by investors in Cannabis 2.0 include unproven management teams, companies with questionable accounting and internal controls, an industry without any financial or banking systems, and more. For these risks, a cannabis industry investor's calculus requires above average returns to compensate them for the inherent risk of investing in this emerging, federally illegal trade.

So, the cannabis industry in 2019 Q1 was edgy, young, sexy, fun, and the valuations were insane. The industry barely existed five years earlier. There were no veterans. Entrepreneurs and investors alike were trying to figure it out, building the plane in flight. No one thought far enough ahead to even worry about how to land the damn thing. Guess they'll cross that bridge when the fuel runs low. (**Author's note:** as of 2020 Q1, the fuel is running low.)

Since everyone wanted to be a part of this industry, capital was plentiful, and Cannabis 2.0 company valuations soared, peaking in 2018 Q4. It was like the Dot.com era all over again (and we all know what happened when that bubble burst in 2001). The most insane stock in the September 2018 time period was a stock called Tilray. Having gone public in July 2018 at about $20 per share, I first noticed the stock on CNBC's *Squawk Box* crawl in late August. In under two weeks, Tilray's stock went from $45 to $80 to $110 to about $140 — and then in *one crazy day* in mid-September, the stock more than doubled to $300 per share. For a few hours, at least, Tilray, which would end the year with only about $40 million of revenue, had a market capitalization of about $25 billion, or about *60x revenues!* Insane. Tilray's bubble popped, and the stock soon returned to the $140s and finished 2018 in the $70 range. As of December 2019, Tilray stock is trading around $20 per share. Pop goes the bubble!

> It's always fun to speculate what a $10,000 investment would be worth if you bought at the lowest and sold at the highest. In the case of Tilray, you would have netted $2.8 million in just three months, an annualized return of over 100,000%. Good work if you could get it and certainly a life changing event.

The market was frenzied. Valuations were frothy. They get this way when emotions and hype take the place of disciplined financial investment. In a frenzied market, people get burned (usually the retail investor and inexperienced, arrogant management teams). MSOs were now bidding against each other and chasing acquisition targets at prices that can only be described as *stupid*, as they defied any rational market theory.

Our company was undisciplined with respect to acquisitions, often shooting from the hip. I'm quite sure that Greg, whose official title was Chief Growth Officer (whatever that means), never put pen to paper in valuing companies. He wouldn't know how. He wouldn't understand how the companies he was chasing faired vis-à-vis the traditional financial metrics such as Return on Investment (ROI), Internal Rate of Return (IRR), Discounted Cash Flow (DCF), or Net Present Value (NPV) if his life depended on it. He was a kid on a spending spree with other people's money, unaware of the consequences of shareholder dilution, and unable to quantify it.

The only metric he used to gauge if he was offering too much for a company was what the competition was offering. As long as the competitors were offering $X, then he would need to offer $X+$1 to bag the deal. He lived in the moment. He had no forethought as to how the ridiculous prices he was offering for acquisitions would ultimately lead to the train wreck that the industry would find itself in less than a year later. Cannabis "executives" like Greg are a big reason why many Cannabis 2.0 companies are running out of cash and are on life support as of 2020 Q1.

Soon, undisciplined companies whose strategy was to plant as many flags as possible in their geographic footprint maps (at whatever cost) were offering 2, 3, 4, even 5x the annual revenue to purchase single dispensaries and grow centers. Insane pricing, but not to these young entrepreneurs, because *they didn't know what they don't know*. To them, this was business as usual, the price of poker. Mom-and-pop dispensary and grow operators (and their children, grandchildren, and great grandchildren) who were able to sell their companies to these MSOs for cash at these stupid valuations are about the only winners in the Cannabis 2.0 era. They benefitted from the inexperience of these C-suite executives who were giddy doing deals using their "gut instincts." These mom-and-pop sellers will be laughing all the way to the bank for generations to come because Cannabis 2.0 C-suite executives were cannibalizing their own companies' shareholder value to add more pins to their geographic footprint maps.

DIRTY LITTLE SECRET #1

THE CANNABIS INDUSTRY IS A CROSS BETWEEN *GREEN ACRES AND THE WILD, WILD WEST*

You would think that with all the publicity and interest in the cannabis industry that it would be a case-study in efficiency. Think again.

Did you ever watch *Green Acres*? It was a '60s sitcom in which a couple from Manhattan gives up their Park Avenue lifestyle and moves to a farm. The husband, Oliver Wendell Douglas, an attorney who wanted to be a farmer, dragged Lisa, his Melania Trump-like high maintenance wife, kicking and screaming away from her world of entitlement.

They move to the absurdist world of Hooterville and its oddball *Hootervillian* residents, such as Mr. Drucker, Mr. Kimball, Mr. Haney, Eb, the Ziffels (including Arnold, their talking pig), and more. The conflict in the show is that Mr. Douglas is the only one (along with the audience who breaks through television's fourth wall) who understands 1+1=2, whereas the rest of the characters and all of Hooterville, including Lisa, believe 1+1=3. Every episode of the oddball Hooterville world challenged Mr. Douglas and the constructs of reality.

Cannabis 2.0 feels a lot like Hooterville, where the business concepts and norms embedded in the reality of other industries just don't matter. The cannabis gold rush smacks of the Dot.com era in which all bets were off. Salaries were inflated. Rents were amplified. Titles and experience were exaggerated. People who were, at best, mid-level managers in the corporate world were suddenly "all knowing" C-level executives in the Wild West of the internet . . . and they worked for "entrepreneurs" who previously never worked for anyone before at all. This worked for a short time until the Dot.com crash that began in early 2001. In retrospect, the Dot.com era was a time of wild valuations, the great unknown, and fortunes won and lost. A lot of paper million and billionaires for sure. It reminded the world about speculative bubbles, bubbles that would recur in 2008 with the mortgage and real estate crisis, and then again in 2018 with digital currencies like Bitcoin. Again, fortunes won and lost. Is the cannabis industry also a bubble? The cannabis industry circa 2020 Q1 has all the indications that the bubble has already burst.

What about the folks who are running today's cannabis companies? Lawyers, small business owners, and low-level managers from corporate America disproportionately populate the C-suites. In all cases, other than their high school and college research in marijuana, what do they know about running a cannabis company? The simple truth about the cannabis industry is that *nobody knows*. This is virgin territory without any history. Everyone is a pioneer like Lewis and Clark. Think Dot.com redux. Everyone is figuring it out as the industry is developing. Regulators, entrepreneurs, bankers, investors, and other stakeholders are trying to figure it out on the fly.

When you take a job in corporate America, guard rails regarding norms of professional behavior, what is possible, what is taboo, etc. exist. In the cannabis industry, by contrast, no rules or rulebooks exist. Everyone brings with them their own experiences and capabilities into the ever-changing incubator of this promising, but Wild West, industry. There are a lot of young cowboys. There are a lot of fools. The executive talent is scarce when it comes to their experience in consolidating and integrating the industry's disparate mom-and-pop companies into cohesive larger, profitable, and in some cases, public companies.

Hundreds of entrepreneurs in the cannabis industry got their start by applying for, winning, and, maybe even, commencing operations at a dispensary or cultivation/grow facility. That said, the talent funnel narrows significantly in that fewer than a couple of dozen entrepreneurs were able to cobble together some operating companies and dispensaries in multiple states to work towards an RTO and run a public company. Still fewer have the chops or experience to be successful in this endeavor.

The natural maturation process often found in consolidating industries includes moving from the growth-stifling chaos customarily found in an industry's Version 1.0 state to a Version 2.0 state in which sophisticated capital and experienced management enter the industry. In turn, these factors allow the enterprise to achieve scale and efficiencies through the implementation of proven systems, basic internal controls and financial reporting, best practices, standard operating procedures, and a framework for corporate governance that these experienced professionals bring with them.

At the start of 2018, the cannabis industry predominantly found itself in this consolidation stage. Strategic investor Constellation Brands (famous for brands like Corona and Modelo) sent shockwaves through the cannabis industry when it made a considerable bet in October 2018 by investing $4 *billion* into Canopy Growth. With this kind of investment, things get serious quickly. Valuations across the industry skyrocketed overnight. However, within nine months and with losses of nearly $100 million in 2019 Q2 alone, Bruce Linton, Canopy's CEO, was shown the door. Losses at Canopy continued to mount through 2019 Q4. As the industry moves to Cannabis 3.0, he certainly won't be the last early-stage cannabis industry CEO to be fired.

As evidence of how markets react when a CEO with Fortune 500 experience and serious credentials enters Cannabis 2.0, consider that in December 2019, Canopy Growth announced that Constellation Brands' *CFO* would become Canopy Growth's new *CEO*. Hiring an experienced CFO to replace its previous CEO signaled Canopy is serious about transition-ing from the Wild West to becoming a profitable company. Not surprisingly, Canopy Growth's stock popped a whopping 14% in one day as investors endorsed this move.

As with any industry in a consolidation stage, like the waste manage-ment industry beginning in the late '70s, the equipment rental industry start-ing in the '90s, or the freight brokerage industry of the 2010s, consolidation tends to attract proven management who bring their systems, processes, and experience in running large enterprises with them. Consolidation also attracts "smart money," which demands disciplined corporate governance, evaluation of the management team, and stellar financial and operational reporting. Smart money also expects economies of scale to be exploited along with the implementation of cost controls. Smart money is more demanding and exerts more influence at the Board of Directors level. It is almost a given that those inexperienced but scrappy entrepreneurs who have bootstrapped their busi-nesses with nothing more than a "never take no for an answer" passion for making something out of nothing will be roadkill and collateral damage as they don't have the experience to take their companies to the proverbial "next level." (**Author's note:** I've raised capital for many companies in many indus-tries. The standard line that looks good in these capital raise pitch decks and discussions is, "We're looking for *smart money*." With that said, when too many companies say, "We're not interested," and cash is running out, *dumb money* looks pretty good as well!)

In the early stages of a corporation's growth, it is probably an advantage that an entrepreneur has never worked for anyone before. They never experi-enced the red tape, corporate bureaucracy, and other corporate customs that can slow down or even halt company growth.

On the other hand, entrepreneurs who have never worked for anybody other than themselves quickly become a liability. The reason? As the com-pany continues to grow, they just don't have the requisite corporate experi-ence necessary to run large enterprises. The shortcuts that helped them in the private world are huge liabilities in public companies or private companies with many investors. They don't know all the "rules" and end up putting the company, themselves, employees, and shareholders in situations that they should never be in, often betting the proverbial farm. By both definition and necessity, these gun-slingers will be weeded out as the industry matures into Cannabis 3.0.

Cannabis: A case study in capitalism

Part of the attraction for seasoned executives in joining young companies in young industries is the ability to participate in the upside for growing shareholder value. That's one of the underpinnings of capitalism: shareholder value (i.e., wealth) creation. To be clear, *for-profit* companies are not in business to save the world, reduce their carbon footprint, employ people, or solve world peace. No. The primary goal of *for-profit* companies is to increase shareholder value. Period. Everything else is a by-product.

Consider Walmart. With over 2.3 million employees, Walmart is the largest U.S. employer, but not because that was its goal. It is the largest employer only by necessity as a by-product of its business model. If it could employ only one million employees and deliver the same shareholder value, it would. Everything it does, from charitable giving to setting associates' wages, is financially modeled. Its actions and policies are the formulaic result of solving the complex linear programming equation that maximizes shareholder value.

Arguably, the United States has the best quality of life (i.e., running water, electricity [except, of late, during the fire season in California], food, jobs, income, etc.) for its citizens largely because of private sector capitalism. When the folks in Silicon Valley, or wherever, make millions it is because they develop products, services, or technologies that people want and which increase our standard of living. We should applaud their success. You know, *To the victor go the spoils.*

No doubt, there is a fair amount of luck involved in being in the right-place at the right-time; but, in general, a capitalistic society is highly efficient in allocating resources and rewarding those with initiative, hustle, and good ideas — much more efficient than, oh, let's say, government entities. The government should be smaller, not larger! For this reason, we should not confiscate the wealth of successful entrepreneurs by enacting things like wealth taxes on the *uber* wealthy. We should be careful not to fall down the slippery slope of socialism, which destroys incentives for inventors and risk takers who have provided the world with the things that we can't live without: from railroads and cars to computers and smart phones. With the U.S. already over $20 *trillion* in debt, I'm not sure sending more money to Washington D.C. is the answer. Don't get me started.

Such is the case with the cannabis industry. A lot of fortunate folks who saw an opportunity to, for example, apply for one of the thousands of state cannabis licenses. And what differentiates them from a lot of wannabes is that these folks put their own capital at risk. They didn't just talk a good game. They risked their capital by writing checks, sometimes even mortgaging their homes, and providing personal guarantees should the shit hit the fan. And that is why entrepreneurs and business owners deserve the fruits of their efforts *uncapped.* They are not a piggy bank for politicians to break open when times are tough.

The lucky ones who won these licenses now had something of value. Many of them were able to assemble the necessary capital stack (from family and friends and other investors, but not from FDIC-backed banks prohibited from loaning money for activities that are still deemed to be federally illegal) to open their first dispensaries or cultivation centers. (An average cost of about $250 thousand to $1 million for a dispensary and $10 to $15 million for a cultivation center.) After winning a cannabis license, many entrepreneurs won't have the contacts or knowledge for how to assemble the additional capital needed to open their businesses and turn their licenses into a cash-flowing operation. And so, instead of opening their businesses, they embarked on the path to sell their licenses to others. The prices of these licenses skyrocketed in the second half of 2018, fueled, in part, by indications that big alcohol, tobacco, and pharma companies would provide the ultimate exit strategies for these fledgling cannabis businesses.

I know of many dispensary *licenses* (i.e., licenses only, the business was not even opened) that were sold for $5 million to $10 million or more in Cannabis 2.0! Not bad for mom-and-pops filling out some paperwork around the kitchen table. In a cannabis industry extreme, licenses in Florida are probably the most expensive. Florida, grants licenses in a vertically integrated package: one grow/cultivation facility and up to thirty dispensaries. (In the Florida model, unlike most other states, you can only sell what you grow to your own licensed dispensaries.) A single license in Florida was worth around $50 - $60 million in 2018 Q4. Keep in mind that after winning a license in Florida, the fun is just beginning. You still need the capital to build-out thirty dispensaries at about $500 thousand each and build a grow/cultivation facility at about $10 million. So, all told, to play in Florida would cost $75 - $85 million. Remember, since traditional debt financing is generally not available, one would have to raise that much in equity. If you are lucky, you might be able to find alternative lenders with convertible notes and the like to help minimize shareholders' dilution. But cannabis industry lenders, if you can find them, will extract their pound of flesh one way or another through usurious interest rates usually accompanied by stock warrants.

> Stock warrants provide lenders an extra incentive (i.e., an equity sweetener), giving them the right to buy shares later on at an agreed (usually lower) price.

Monopoly money

I am familiar with one cannabis company that bought a vertically integrated medical marijuana license in Florida for $100 million in an all stock deal. Yes, $100 million! At the time, the going rate for licenses in Florida were in the $50 - $60 million range. Why, then, would this company pay almost a 100% premium to grab a license in Florida? I'm not sure there is a rational answer. (I feel like Mr. Douglas on *Green Acres* here.) The explanations (disguised as a well-thought-out strategy) given by the Hootervillian management team at this company include:

- "Over-paying will reduce our time to market;"
- "It is part of a convoluted three-way transaction in which we will raise $100 million cash;"
- "With this transaction, it makes us a player in the industry and puts us on the map."

My favorite explanation for paying lofty prices for cannabis acquisition companies that I hear quite a bit in the industry is: "Who cares, we're paying with stock, and that's just *Monopoly money.*" Yep. I heard this with my own ears. To my investor audience: when you hear your CEO rationalize paying a 100% premium to the market for a license and then justifying the transaction because it is being paid in stock, this is a strong indication that the "executive" team *doesn't know what it doesn't know.* They have never seriously calculated the effects of dilution. Ask to see their models underpinning their rosy projections. Don't be surprised if they never put pencil to paper to rationalize the purchase price premium they paid with *Monopoly money* — a.k.a. Shareholder money. They are shooting from the hip in the Wild, Wild West.

COMPANY A: A CANNABIS LAND GRAB AND $30 MILLION SWEPT UNDER THE RUG

Doug, the founder of Company A, was a go-getter with unbridled energy. In short order, and through a very complex ownership structure, Company A, like other MSOs, was able to cobble together about a half-dozen operating companies in several states. Like most entrepreneurs, Doug can attribute his success to 50% luck and 50% high energy hustle. (**Author's note:** I've seen many entrepreneurs who were always lucky: they seemed to have the lucky golden horseshoe in everything they do; on the flipside, I've seen entrepreneurs who couldn't get *lucky* in a women's prison!)

That said, Doug really shit the bed on a few transactions. When it came to acquisitions, Doug lacked experience and strategy and didn't understand the importance of performing thorough due diligence. Due diligence is the equivalent of "kicking the tires" when evaluating whether or not to buy a used car. It is a critical part of the acquisition process. Shareholders assume their management teams perform thorough due diligence before consummating a transaction. (Bad assumption in Cannabis 2.0.) Doug lacked a sound strategy when it came to looking for acquisitions. He was 90% opportunistic and 10% strategic. He wanted to buy anything that came in over the transom.

My experience in managing the M&A activity of a $13 billion division of a Fortune 100 company suggests that Doug's "acquisition strategy approach" was really not an acquisition strategy at all. It was sophomoric at best. (***Author's note:*** In college, while working on a group project, I was told that my ideas were "sophomoric." Because I was only a freshman at the time, I took that as a complement.)

Paying what the competition is willing to pay inevitably leads to a bidding war in which the seller most always wins, and the acquiring company's shareholders most always lose. It is a technique used in "land grab" opportunities (prevalent in consolidating industries) in which companies go out and grab as much "real estate" (in this case, licenses and operating cannabis assets) as quickly as possible. Companies and investors look past high purchase prices and lack of immediate profitability, betting that growth in the industry will hopefully provide the runway necessary to achieve enormous profits once economies of scale are realized. The thinking is that in two or three years, they will look back and say, "What a steal that was at the price we paid." There are examples where a land grab has proven to be a great strategy, and it forever cements the dominance of large players in specific industries.

Of course, a successful land grab strategy assumes that the management team knows how to integrate disparate acquisitions, operate them efficiently, and squeeze out duplicative costs. They must also calculate the capital needed to soldier through the years of cash losses until they achieve positive cash flow. In executing a land grab strategy, patient investors are also a necessity, and company management should make a point to over-communicate with them, keeping them fully-informed through regular and fully transparent communications. As seen in Cannabis 2.0, paying ridiculous prices for acquisitions has sobering consequences: companies' valuations have taken a dump, and many once high-flyers are running short on cash in 2020 Q1.

One entrepreneur who has successfully executed land grab strategies in several industries is Bradley Jacobs. I was lucky enough to have worked for this world-class entrepreneur in the early '90s. I was the third executive on-board his waste-industry start-up, United Waste Systems, in 1990. Having a front row seat and learning from the best, we ended up taking that company public just two years later in 1992. Then, only five short years after that, United Waste Systems was sold for $2 *billion*. Bradley now had street credentials. The best kind of street cred: *Wall Street* cred. Bradley had the "chops" and was now a player. Wall Street firms lined up to throw money at Bradley in his next venture . . .

. . . which, as it turned out, was starting United Rentals, and which, through a *disciplined* acquisition strategy, quickly became the largest equipment rental company in the world (United Rentals' 2018 revenues are around $8 billion). As successful as these companies were, Bradley didn't stop there. Bradley's latest home-run is having turned a fledgling freight company into one of the largest freight logistics company in the world: XPO Logistics, with 2018 revenues of over $17 billion. I'm sure you've seen the United Rental and XPO Logistics logos everywhere.

For the first several years, XPO didn't turn a profit. Bradley didn't care. His strategy was that of a land grab. He cast his net into different niches of the logistics industry and planted seeds that would one day bear fruit, losing money for several years along the way. Because of his past successes, Wall Street and the markets were patient with Bradley. While XPO wasn't initially profitable, XPO Logistics' stock stayed strong regardless, because, unlike today's cannabis executives, Bradley had a track record and was bankable. He was a known quantity. The markets knew he would deliver, and he did.

As an irrefutable testament to Bradley's genius, *both* United Rentals' and XPO Logistics' stocks were in the *top twenty* of the *Best Performing Stocks of the Decade (i.e., the 2010s).*[7] United Rentals came in at #15 (1564% growth) and XPO Logistics came in at #17 (1530% growth). Not one, but two stocks of companies that Bradley Jacobs started were "10-baggers," growing over 10-fold during the decade.

Two companies in the top twenty — that's unheard of, world-class performance.

In three major public companies in three different industries, Bradley has successfully completed over five hundred acquisitions with a disciplined acquisition strategy. He knows what to pay for companies and when to walk away. He doesn't guess. He isn't emotional. He is no flash in the pan. He is world-class.

But too often, inexperienced entrepreneurs believe they are Bradley Jacobs-caliber, who can pull off a land grab strategy by acquiring companies at any cost. The cannabis industry is full of these guys. The problem is that they overpay and don't even know that they do it. They don't realize the time value of money, capital markets, and the like. They all promise to be profitable "next year," but next year never comes. They never do the math. They don't know when to walk away. They are no Bradley Jacobs.

The *Harvard Business Review* is full of empirical studies from quantitative financial jocks, which conclude that shareholders of companies that habitually overpay for acquisitions as measured by sound financial measures like Discounted Cash Flow (DCF) and Return on Investment (ROI) are rarely rewarded. It's no wonder that with managers like these acting as fiduciaries for shareholders that 60% of M&A deals destroy shareholder value. And this is what has happened in 2019 in the cannabis industry.

Further, in a recent Grant Thornton survey of four-hundred executives less than a third of participants say their company had a "clear, understood M&A strategy."[8] It is more likely than not that the folks running today's cannabis companies, many of whom have no meaningful corporate business experience and little to no acquisitions experience, don't have a clue as to whether or not the prices they are paying for acquisitions create or destroy shareholder value. They're winging it and maybe with your money! Cowboys.

In the cannabis land grab during 2018 Q4, many cannabis executives made, in retrospect, some rookie mistakes, including paying four to five times the annual revenue for certain dispensaries and licenses. The immediate proof of these mistakes is that the cannabis industry in 2020 Q1 is trading at less than half what it was only a year ago, and these companies continue to burn through cash. Many companies' survival is in question thanks to bad management, poor decision-making, and flawed strategy that contributes to racking up huge and unsustainable cash losses.

For ease and simplicity, cannabis industry executives value companies using the back of the envelope multiples of *revenue* instead of the more superior method, multiples of *profitability* or of *cash flow proxies* like Earnings Before Interest, Taxes, Depreciation, and Amortization (EBITDA).

> EBITDA is a quick down and dirty proxy used for how much cash a company is generating. Valuing companies based on a multiple of EBITDA is, itself, a shortcut for the more rigorous DCF or ROI analysis, but it is preferred to using multiples of revenue, as is common in the cannabis industry.

When industries use multiples of revenue instead of multiples of EBITDA in valuing a company, it is a pretty good bet that the industry and company management teams are either a) executing a land grab strategy (that focuses on revenue growth, not caring about profitability or cash flow), b) unsophisticated, c) not profitable (which makes multiples of EBITDA not meaningful), or d) all of the above. Such is the case in Cannabis 2.0.

Back to Company A. Doug started negotiations with a California-based acquisition target under the belief that the acquisition target had $30 million in annual revenue. As is typical in the cannabis industry and other industries in a land grab consolidation phase, many management teams have minimal regard for due diligence, despite having a fiduciary responsibility to their shareholders. Worse yet, in deals structured as stock acquisitions (in which the company is purchasing the stock of a target in an acquisition as opposed to only buying certain assets of a target company), the company is not only purchasing the assets of the company but also its *liabilities — whether known or unknown!* So, it is prudent that companies conduct thorough due diligence in the acquisition process. In Cannabis 2.0, *rigorous due diligence* is a lesser priority than *speed* in locking acquisitions up under Letters of Intent (LOI), which outline the broad terms of an acquisition between buyer and seller.

In his haste to strike while the market was hot, Doug almost always rushed to enter into a Letter of Intent to purchase a company using the simple, multiple of revenue-based valuation and not much more than that. Don't worry about the details. This is what cowboys do. In the case of the $30 million acquisition, he quickly negotiated a purchase price of $90 million, or 3x revenue with the seller. Doug instructed Company A's attorneys to prepare the LOI. They would (hopefully) perform due diligence before the deal was finalized and memorialized in a document commonly referred to as the Definitive Agreement.

The problem occurred after they entered into the Letter of Intent. Instead of diving deep into the due diligence, Doug was off to lock up other acquisitions. Company A's management was stretched thin and did not have an acquisitions department and certainly lacked the bench strength to conduct thorough due diligence on acquisition targets, a dereliction of fiduciary responsibility to its shareholders. A month goes by since the Letter of Intent was signed, and Company A's CFO finally has the opportunity to perform some cursory due diligence before the parties enter into the Definitive Agreement. By diving deep into the details, complicated ownership structure, and the various intercompany management fees and other transactions, the CFO uncovered a material issue: the net "consolidateable" revenue under Generally Accepted Accounting Principles (GAAP) was not the $30 million as Doug believed, but was instead only $20 million! Had that been known upfront, the LOI would have been negotiated for 3x $20 million or $60 million, not $90 million. This meant Doug's offer for this acquisition was $30 million or 50% more than it would have been had the correct revenues been known upfront. *Missed it by that much!* But why sweat the details?

It turned out that the same day that Company A's CFO uncovered this rather material fact, Doug had a dinner planned with the seller to enter into the binding Definitive Agreement. The CFO called Doug that afternoon to say, "Hey Doug, I just uncovered a material error in your valuation of the target company. Their revenues are only $20 million, not $30 million, as you previously thought. I'm sure glad I won't be at that dinner tonight as it will be a bit uncomfortable when you have to explain and renegotiate the price to $60 million. Good luck."

The next day, the CFO asked Doug how the seller responded to the renegotiated price. Doug replied, "Oh, we just left the purchase price the same."

Wait; what?

Excuse me? Are you kidding me? *Are you kidding me?* Doug was going to leave the purchase price the same, and he was content sweeping a $30 million error under the rug? (The purchase price would now equate to 5x revenues.) This is the same CEO who mandated Company A employees not spend more than $100 per night for a hotel when they travel (good luck when traveling to New York, San Francisco, or just about any place in between, even in fly-over country). Yet, he let a $30 million error go uncorrected? Was he going to hide this *faux pas* from Company A's investors and Board of Directors? In his eagerness to show growth and additional acquisitions, Doug just moved on to the next acquisition as if nothing had happened. Effectively, $30 million of shareholder value vaporized. Doug's shareholders were none the wiser: they never received communication or updates from the company. Doug ran Company A as he previously ran his own privately-held company without shareholders. He was accountable only to himself. *But it's only Monopoly money, remember?*

And this is why investors demand a risk premium in the cannabis industry: to protect them from real and material mistakes of inexperienced management who ignore their fiduciary responsibility to their shareholders. Because Company A was still privately-held with an ineffective Board of Directors, there was really no oversight or transparency to speak of, and the investors would forever be in the dark as to this colossal mistake. Kind of makes saving a few shekels on hotel stays an exercise in futility. Only in Hooterville!

Company B: Board oversight?

You might ask, "Didn't Company A have a Board of Directors to review and police the actions of its officers?" Great question! I'll let you in on a secret: The Boards of Directors at many Cannabis 2.0 companies don't even meet and they are stuffed with insiders whose interests are not aligned with the non-insider shareholders. In Cannabis 2.0, the fox routinely guards the henhouse.

Take the case of Company B. Its Board consisted of five individuals: two founders, one Chief Legal Officer (the insiders), and two Board Members from earlier acquisitions. Only one person on the Board had any experience working in medium to large companies. None of them had experience being on Boards representing many shareholders, none truly understood what *fiduciary responsibility* means, and there was a substantial conflict between looking out for their self-interest and self-dealing and those interests of the non-insider shareholders whose money was integral in fueling the growth of the company. Unfortunately, this is the rule rather than the exception in the cannabis industry. Fiduciary, my ass!

These Cannabis 2.0 Boards don't provide the level of oversight that shareholders expect and to which they are accustomed. Outside of Hooterville, investors rightfully expect their Board of Directors to meet regularly, minimally quarterly, to review results, assess management talent, and plot strategy. Detailed minutes are taken which carefully document what was discussed and agreed to at the Board meetings. Not so much in the cannabis industry. Company B's Board didn't even meet in the past year. When Company B needed formal approval from its Board to be acquired, they hastily arranged a telephonic Board meeting with minimal advance notice. Requisite materials related to the proposed transaction were not distributed in advance for the Board members to review before casting their votes. (***Author's note:*** This is kind of like how the U.S. House Judiciary Committee operates its impeachment inquiry: thousands of pages of material dumped on members of Congress with less than 48 hours to review the documents. Where's Evelyn Wood when you need her?)

It probably didn't matter if materials were provided to Company B's Board in advance anyway because the Board vote was just a formality in that the insiders had the voting power to do whatever they wanted. (Again, much like the U.S. House Judiciary Committee. The impeachment hearings were strictly window dressing, Kabuki theater. The outcome of the House of Representatives' impeachment vote was already a *fait accompli.*)

Company B's Board lacked teeth. It was a joke. Unfortunately, Company B's example of poor corporate governance seems to be the rule rather than the exception in the cannabis industry. The fox guards the henhouse.

COMPANY C: LACK OF DUE DILIGENCE — A $4 MILLION MISTAKE

Here's another interesting story regarding the lack of due diligence, management being caught with their pants down, and their participation in a scheme to screw certain owners of an acquisition target. This can only happen in Hooterville.

Like some other young cannabis entrepreneurs, the young founders/owners of Company C always gravitated to shiny objects: celebrities, parties, publicity, you name it. They came across a company they wanted to acquire, and the target company was majority-owned (75%) by Mary, the girlfriend of a famous Las Vegas-based movie industry insider with a checkered past. Two other investors owned the other 25% of Mary's company.

Company C's founders were having fun hanging out with these peeps. They discussed buying Mary's company, and she presented a brief financial statement to them showing her company having $6 million of revenue. That's it. It was one-page. With this one-page unaudited financial statement, the Company C owners offered about $3 million for 40% of Mary's company. But, in true cannabis industry greed, Mary did not want to share the proposed purchase price with her two other partners. So, Company C's owners and Mary structured a scheme to secretly subsidize Mary while circumventing her fellow shareholders. The deal was structured such that Company C would pay $100,000 for 40% of the company's equity. This nominal amount was to be shared proportionately by Mary and her partners. However, unbeknownst to Mary's other two equity partners, Company C entered into a separate consulting agreement with Mary for $3 million to be paid to her in twenty-four monthly installments. So, this would be their little secret . . . at least that was the plan.

While Mary and the Company C founders hoped that Mary's other shareholders would never learn about her lucrative consulting agreement, they were all naïve when it came to the routine disclosures that would be required as part of Company C's audit. (A $3 million consulting contract is material, and Company C would have to disclose the particulars of this agreement.) Of course, Company C management didn't realize this because *they didn't know what they don't know.* They never ran across the need to disclose consulting contracts in their previous small-business lives.

With Company C's help, Mary would garner the benefit of a nearly $3 million payday while she and her other shareholders sold 40% of her company for a pittance. I'm not sure that this transaction is illegal, but at the very least, it is highly unethical. What would Mary's other minority equity partners say if they knew that the reason Mary encouraged them to approve the paltry $100,000 transaction was that she would benefit handsomely from a lucrative, secretive side-deal? Wouldn't they get curious when they see Mary driving a Lamborghini? Is this how Cannabis 2.0 executives act to bag another acquisition? Do they have any ethics? Didn't Company C's Board have to review and approve all acquisitions?

Ooops. There was something else. In their haste to bag Mary's company, Company C's founders didn't realize that the $3 million in payments structured as "consulting expense" would torpedo the EBITDA amount they projected to their investors, thus shooting themselves in the foot with respect to trying to maximize Company C's valuation. EBIT*DUH!* Of course, Company C's founders never reviewed the particulars of this transaction with their CFO, in part, because they didn't want him to discover the details of their scheme with Mary.

The story takes still another turn, not surprisingly for the worse. Remember that the owners of Company C thought they bought a company with $6 million of revenue. As it turned out, this wasn't the case. Mary visited Company C's California headquarters a few months after the acquisition. Company C's Chief Operating Officer asked Mary for more details regarding the products that the newly acquired company sold. Mary provided the COO additional data from *QuickBooks*, a popular accounting software used in the industry. The data showed about fifty or so products' (SKUs) sales for the past six months.

Interestingly to the COO, the total sales for the most recent six-month period were only about $600 thousand, implying annual revenue of $1.2 million, not the $6 million Mary had previously represented. The COO asked John, Company C's CFO, "I thought the company we acquired had revenues of $6 million? Mary just showed me a report stating annual revenues of about $1.2 million. What gives?"

John immediately dropped what he was doing to look into the issue as he, too, was told by Company C's owners that the acquisition's revenues were $6 million. Only in Hooterville, in the absence of due diligence, are mistakes like this are uncovered *after* an acquisition has been consummated. In the real world, these misrepresentations are vetted in due diligence early in the process, and the acquisition is scrapped before wasting significant Company C resources. Like Company A that swept a $30 million error under the rug, if Company C had performed the most cursory of due diligence, it would have discovered that the $6 million as reported by Mary was, at best, inaccurate, and at worst, fraudulent.

John confronted Mary, who confessed that the $6 million financial statement included cash sales, which never made its way to the bank, or the company's income tax return. Instead, the partners pocketed the cash sales outside the auspices of the IRS.

"So, let me get this straight," John queried Mary, "we bought 40% of a company that has filed fraudulent tax returns (a felony), and on a go-forward basis we will not realize revenues of $6 million but instead, only $1.2 million a year? Do you see anything wrong here?" Mary was speechless. It was at this point that she realized she would most likely never see a dime from her $3 million consulting agreement.

As in the story of the young, inexperienced Company A management team, John had to educate Company C's founders as to his findings. John called the founders into his office. He tried to be tactful, but educating these founders on fiduciary responsibility, ethics, and internal controls was a never-ending task. His talk quickly turned into a full-blown rant: "How can this happen? How can you strike a deal with Mary's company thinking you're acquiring and paying for $6 million of revenue when it only has about $1 million of revenue? Where was your due diligence? More importantly, how can you put the company *and its shareholders* in jeopardy by stepping into a potentially huge criminal tax liability? And what are you going to do to correct this? Are you going to continue to pay Mary her monthly fee according to her consulting contract? Are you going to the IRS and turn her in? What are you going to do? And, while we're at it, how could you conspire with Mary to, effectively, screw her other shareholders?" Company C's founders were speechless. Eventually, they tried to minimize John's concerns. One of them said, "John, you're acting as though you're not a fan of this transaction." John replied, "I'm not acting."

If these Company C founders were like the founders in Company A, they probably looked the other way with their shareholders none the wiser. More millions of dollars wasted by incompetent, inexperienced managers. But that's okay; *it's only Monopoly money, right?*

COMPANY D: DIRECTORS AND OFFICERS (D&O) INSURANCE —WHERE ART THOU?

Another necessity for companies in *hypergrowth* industries is providing insurance to protect their directors and officers from lawsuits. This insurance is aptly named "D&O" insurance for the directors and officers it seeks to pro-tect. For most companies, including companies in relatively mature but bor-ing industries like food service or manufacturing, D&O insurance is readily available and relatively affordable. As a datapoint, companies can purchase $25 million of coverage with relatively low deductibles (say, $250,000) for an annual premium of $100,000. Mature industries are usually comprised of seasoned companies with sterling reputations and sterling Boards that take their fiduciary responsibilities to their shareholders and other stakeholders seriously. As such, the incidents of shareholder lawsuits for which insurance companies would need to pay millions of dollars in claims are few and far between, and since D&O insurance premiums reflect risk, these policies are relatively affordable in mature industries.

The cannabis industry, however, is anything but mature and boring. For the cannabis industry, D&O insurance is either prohibitively expensive or, if companies can obtain it at all, it is so watered down that it is not worth the paper on which it is written. Several factors illustrate why this is the case.

First, people with no previous corporate experience lead many Cannabis 2.0 companies. They are cowboys in the Wild West. Insurance company underwriters know this even if the executives don't. Further, while many cannabis company CEOs and leaders are inexperienced, many are out-right unscrupulous. In underwriting and pricing D&O insurance, the insur-ance companies will seek to understand the company's "tone at the top." In other words, do the leaders of these companies operate their businesses ethically and with integrity? Are they forthcoming and transparent? Do they understand fiduciary responsibility? Do they conduct due diligence on acqui-sitions? Is the Board controlled by insiders or by a majority of outsiders? Does the Board drive accountability deep into the company, or is it just a rubber stamp? To determine the tone at the top, as part of their underwriting due diligence, the insurance company interviews the management teams seeking to know:

- "What is your previous experience in running companies? Have you been a C-level person in a public company? A VP? Director? Manager?
- Have you ever declared bankruptcy? Has any company in which you served as an officer ever declared bankruptcy?
- Have you ever been on a Board of Directors before? Been sued?"

Because the business of cannabis is very new and still emerging, this Wild West type of industry is ripe for lawsuits. The underwriters give points to those executive teams that have "been there, done that," worked in public companies, been on a Board, etc. all of which indicate that they understand their fiduciary responsibilities. The underwriters try to weed out inexperienced management teams and actors with dubious histories. They try to weed out the "hacks."

Second, the industry is acquisitive and consolidating as opposed to stagnant. In this environment, deals get done quickly, and paperwork, due diligence, and other inconveniences are not always priorities for inexperienced entrepreneurs used to running privately-held companies and not having to provide audit trails (i.e., documentation) for transactions, and not having to act as a fiduciary for shareholders. As such, the parties to an acquisition may not always see eye-to-eye regardless of what agreements are in place and irrespective of whether these agreements are verbal or written. In this environment, the conflict between buyer and seller often leads to litigation and D&O policy payouts.

Third, if the founders or officers lack relevant public company experience, they will most likely continue to run their company as they would their privately-held companies – close to the vest. By contrast, in a public company or a company with many shareholders, you must be transparent; you must disclose related-party transactions and ownership interests in other companies; you must share audited financials with shareholders and regulators. Folks from privately-held businesses aren't used to having teams of auditors and regulators crawl up their ass with magnifying glasses. (***Authors note:***

I'd rather have a proctologist examining my ass instead of an auditor any day, unless, of course, the proctologist has poor depth perception!)

Inexperienced CEOs are skeptical of auditors and will try to hide things from them instead of fully disclosing all relevant information. This behavior will slow down or even stop an audit in its tracks. Compare this behavior to that of experienced public company CEOs who act ethically and with full transparency and assume that auditors will eventually know everything the management team knows, no matter how damaging the consequences.

Company D hired a CFO to help take a Multi-State Operator cannabis company public in Canada. On several occasions, he spoke to the young, inexperienced CEO about his need to be "in the know" about ALL that was happening at the company: every acquisition, agreement, contract, employment offer letter, lease, and more. The CFO needs to know ALL of this and more as these documents, contracts, etc. need to be reviewed from an accounting and legal perspective for proper disclosure as required by Generally Accepted Accounting Principles (GAAP). Accounting accruals may be required, audit footnote disclosures may be necessary, and more. Also, sensitive or gray-area items may require further legal and business ethics reviews by legal counsel so as not to mislead investors or, worse yet, regulators. This information is needed to keep the company and its owners, founders, and officers out of legal jeopardy from disgruntled shareholders or employees. Company D's CFO knew that if auditors feel they aren't getting unfettered access to all information from management which they determine is needed for them to conduct an audit and form its audit opinion, that this red-flag can cause the auditors to go "pencils down" and walk off the engagement.

After several incidents in which the CFO was kept out of the loop on important information flow and despite his almost constant counseling and educating of these inexperienced founders, he resigned as CFO.

As you may know, thanks in part to the Enron scandal of the early 2000s and the subsequent enactment of the Sarbanes-Oxley Act, which necessitated public companies to improve and audit their internal controls and increase the transparency of internal information used to run the company, CFOs and CEOs are required to *certify* the truthfulness and accuracy of quarterly and annual financial statements that are prepared by the company. They need to sign their names on the dotted line. CEOs and CFOs can be found personally and criminally liable for falsifying financial statements.

Company D's CFO told the CEO: "I am resigning as CFO now before we are even public because you failed to change your ways. You haven't shown any inclination to act in ways other than when you were a private company CEO. You haven't demonstrated an understanding of how you need to serve as the CEO of a public company. I'm doing you a favor and telling you this now rather than telling you the day before you want me to certify the quarterly or annual financial statements. You haven't shared all of the pertinent information that I need to do my job. You hide too many undocumented "side-deals" from me. I don't get straight answers when I ask straightforward questions. You don't respect your fiduciary responsibility to all shareholders. In short, you don't get it. As such, I would refuse to certify the financial statements because I can't attest to their accuracy or veracity, and so, I must resign."

Due to the CEO's lack of transparency, the CFO certainly felt that he might not be able to certify the financials as and when the CEO would expect him to. In such an environment, the CFO faces the possibility of being sued by shareholders and could also be criminally prosecuted by regulators. It gets worse: Company D was unable to secure D&O insurance meaning that if the company and its officers were sued by shareholders, employees, investors, or regulators, they would not have the "luxury" of insurance to pay for the costs of defending and settling such suits. Without D&O insurance, cannabis companies and their management teams are naked, risking their personal nest eggs should the shit hit the fan. Company D's CFO couldn't continue to take that risk.

Fourth, several high-profile shareholder lawsuits, some for over $150 million, have been filed against Cannabis 2.0 companies making already skittish D&O insurance markets cost prohibitive as premiums ratchet higher with every lawsuit filed. When many cannabis companies began to go public in the Summer of 2018, D&O insurance was still relatively affordable. Companies could purchase $5 million of coverage with a $500,000 deductible for a premium of around $200,000. Fast forward to 2018 Q4: due to many shareholder lawsuits, less than stellar tones at the top of many cannabis companies, and D&O insurance companies exiting from the cannabis industry altogether, cannabis industry D&O premiums skyrocketed, and coverage was watered down. The most coverage that Company D could procure was $2 million, with a $1 million deductible for an annual premium of about $900,000. The three or so remaining insurance companies that provided a D&O product to the cannabis industry were giving it the middle finger and underwriting a product that isn't worth the paper on which it is written. As such, beginning in 2018 Q4, some cannabis companies went without D&O insurance. Without D&O insurance, many excellent potential Board Members told cannabis companies "no thank you" to invitations to join their Board. Like Company D's CFO, they couldn't afford to risk their personal nest eggs.

And, so begins a sort of death spiral: Companies need qualified, experienced Board members to improve all aspects of corporate governance, but because other industry participants failed to operate with integrity, companies couldn't purchase D&O insurance at affordable rates. As such, many quality Board-level candidates say "no thank you," leaving the industry with a dearth of much needed Board expertise and discipline. It's another reason why the cannabis industry has fallen from grace in less than a year.

INTERMISSION #1

UGGGH . . . MARKETING FOLKS.
THE $2 MILLION LOGO!

In general, I'm skeptical of most of the marketing campaigns developed by marketing departments. While I'm typically trying to make payroll and pay the bills, the marketing folks are dreaming up grandiose and expensive marketing campaigns without putting pencil to paper to prove that the funds they request will move the needle and produce an acceptable return on the investment. Here's one of my favorite stories from the Dot.com era.

At the end of 1999, I was CFO of a Dot.com company that received $15 million in funding. Money was plentiful as everyone wanted to get into this new thing called the internet. The money was raised quickly in about two weeks from a "leafy" twelve-page PowerPoint presentation. As with today's cannabis industry, there wasn't a lot of due diligence by Dot.com investors at the time. Instead, there was a Fear of Missing Out (FOMO) giddiness in the market as investors were quick to place their bets on the roulette table knowing that they would come up with goose eggs in most of these investments, but hoping that at least one of their bets would hit it big. That was the mentality of the Dot.com era, which has resurfaced in Cannabis 2.0.

But I digress. We hired Susan as our SVP-Marketing, and the company overpaid for her experience like they did for me and all others, but such was the Dot.com industry at the time. Susan was previously a low-level marketing manager in corporate America. She came to me one day and said, "Dean, I need $1 million." Even though this was the Dot.com era, I was still frugal. After all, $1 million was still a significant sum of money. While we raised a total of $15 million, we still had dozens of employees to hire and products to produce. I know. I did the math.

I inquired, "$1 million for what?" Susan said she needed the money in her budget to develop our company's logo. It seemed to me like a lot of money for a logo or creative artwork. *Just saying.* I asked, "$1 million for a logo? Where do you come up with that figure?" Without skipping a beat, and rather matter-of-factly, she said, "It's not that much money in the scheme of things. Lucent Technologies recently spent $3 million on their logo, so this is not out of line."

Insert record screech here: Wait; what?

Let's put things in perspective: Lucent was a multi-billion-dollar, international company with real profits, a real Board of Directors, and seasoned executives. Our company had hardly any sales. We weren't Lucent. But yet, Susan believed that she was *saving* our company $2 million by only needing $1 million to develop our logo. Once again, I felt like Mr. Douglas on *Green Acres!*

Here is how I resolved the logo-development conundrum at our little Dot.com company. I gave Susan $100 and told her to go to the local high school, give it to their art department as a stipend, and ask the students to develop logo concepts.

Long story short: we ended up choosing one of those logos as our company's logo. In my mind, I saved the company $999,900. (**Author's note:** To this day, I still kick myself whenever I think about this because I probably could have gone to the local *grade school* for a $50 stipend!)

I entered the Dot.com era as a very disciplined MBA-Finance, classically trained in the teachings of Fama and Friedman and other Nobel prize winners from the University of Chicago, and well-grounded in the concepts of discounted cash flow, return on investment, capital formation theory, and efficient markets. The Dot.com industry, however, was more like Hooterville: detached from all reality, *in many ways similar to Cannabis 2.0 companies.* I let my guard down and became a Hootervillian myself for a short period. After the Dot.com bubble burst, however, I swore I would never let that happen again, and for the next 18 years, I subscribed, once again, to the tenets of classical finance.

But I discovered that everything I learned as a classically trained MBA would be challenged once again in the Summer of 2018 when I became CFO of a Multi-State Operator cannabis company.

DIRTY LITTLE SECRET #2

STATE MEDICAL MARIJUANA LEGISLATION:
ACT I OF A III ACT PLAY

Let's not kid ourselves, in most states medical marijuana legislation is only Act I of a III Act play, with Act II being the addition of *chronic pain* (an all-encompassing ailment that just about anybody can qualify for), and *opioid replacements* to the medical marijuana act language; and Act III being the implementation of the sexier, and more lucrative, recreational use program.

If you think that states that enact medical marijuana laws, or so-called "Compassionate Care Acts," are doing so out of the goodness of their hearts, think again. The laws, as written, paint the picture that these various states' legislators are comprised of the most compassionate, benevolent souls of all of humankind. Look at this excerpt from the State of Illinois' Compassionate Use of Medical Cannabis Pilot Program Act (circa 2014):

> *State law should make a distinction between the medical and non-medical uses of cannabis. Hence, the purpose of this Act is to protect patients with debilitating medical conditions, as well as their physicians and providers, from arrest and prosecution, criminal and other penalties, and*

property forfeiture if the patients engage in the medical use
of cannabis.[9]

Tugs at my heartstrings. These Illinois legislators seem laser-focused on the welfare of their residents suffering from debilitating medical conditions. It even has a nice ring to it: "Compassionate Use" Blah Blah Act. *Surely* this Compassionate Blah Blah Act has nothing to do with setting the table for potentially legalizing recreational marijuana at a later date. *Right?* After all, it says right there: "state law should make a distinction between the medical and non-medical uses of cannabis." Well, I'm not an attorney, but it sure seems to me that because the Land of Lincoln's Compassionate Care Act is so very deliberate in specifying legalizing cannabis only for medical use, that any thought of using marijuana for recreational or non-medical use, even in the future, is forbidden. It's *verboten* as it says right there in the state statute. Further, the Illinois state statute defines:

> *"Cultivation center" means a facility operated by an orga-*
> *nization or business that is registered by the Department of*
> *Agriculture to perform necessary activities to provide only*
> ***registered medical cannabis dispensing organizations***
> ***with usable medical cannabis.***[10]
> **(emphasis added)**

Again, nice guys to assure us that this is solely a medical program and not some path toward full recreational legalization.

The Rest of the Story

Millions of Americans tuned in daily to listen to radio personality Paul Harvey's unique blend of news and views. He understood that every story had a unique twist that may not always be evident to the listener. He was famous for the phrase *The Rest of the Story* to refer to these nuances that underpinned the main story. If Paul Harvey were alive today, he would no doubt be back after a commercial break with "The Rest of the Story" as it relates to medical marijuana legislation.

Your state may be rolling in dough, but the State of Illinois, where I live, shall I say, *ain't*. So, let's follow the money. Illinois' Compassionate Use Blah Blah Act states:

> **Sec. 20. Compassionate Use of Medical Cannabis Fund.**
>
> *(a) There is created the Compassionate Use of Medical Cannabis Fund in the State treasury to be used exclusively for the direct and indirect costs associated with the implementation, administration, and enforcement of this Act. Funds in excess of the direct and indirect costs associated with the implementation, administration, and enforcement of this Act shall be used to fund crime prevention programs.*
>
> *(b) All monies collected under this Act shall be deposited in the Compassionate Use of Medical Cannabis Fund in the State treasury. All earnings received from investment of monies in the Compassionate Use of Medical Cannabis Fund shall be deposited in the Compassionate Use of Medical Cannabis Fund.*
>
> *(c)* **Notwithstanding any other law to the contrary, the Compassionate Use of Medical Cannabis Fund is not subject to sweeps, administrative charge-backs, <u>or any other fiscal or budgetary maneuver that</u> <u>would in any way transfer any amounts from the</u> <u>Compassionate Use of Medical Cannabis Fund into</u> <u>any other fund of the State.</u>**[11]
>
> **(emphasis added)**

Hmmm . . . what could possibly go wrong here? Now, as Paul Harvey would say, here's *The Rest of the Story:*

I am a lifelong resident of Illinois, this "great state," where four of its last seven governors went to prison. It is a state that is, arguably, the worst run state in U.S. history; a state that is consistently teetering on bankruptcy; a state that can't pay its bills and owes its vendors over $14.7 billion and has over $134 billion (and growing) in unfunded pension liability. Illinois is run not by the governor but, instead, by a dictator named Mike Madigan (the longest-serving leader of any state or federal legislative body in the history of the United States) who hijacked the state from its citizenry back in 1983. It is a state that has more bodies of government than any other state; a state with the second highest property tax rates in the country and whose residents are fleeing to other states in record numbers. With this history, I should believe the State of Illinois when it says the deposits and earnings in the Use of Medical Cannabis Fund cannot be transferred by any other fund in this great state? *Really?* I'm not buying it.

Do you think that this cash-strapped state may have an ulterior motive in implementing medical marijuana other than this charade of benevolence to its residents suffering debilitating diseases? Do you think that possibly, just possibly, the life jacket of an additional revenue stream (as in the past with the lottery, casinos, red-light camera programs, video gaming, and taxes upon taxes upon taxes for cigarettes, alcohol, soft drinks, and gasoline) may tempt lawmakers to transfer funds to any of the Illinois' other money pits? For instance, do you believe that the Illinois pension system is receiving the profits from the state lottery as advertised upon implementation in 1974? Methinks not!

In fact, the system is so broken that not only weren't the pensions getting the profits from the lottery as designed; *even the lottery winners couldn't get paid!* At one time, around 2015, the Illinois lottery *stopped paying winners* and, instead, issued IOUs. The backlog of unpaid winnings was almost $300 million in prize money. Yet, they kept selling lottery tickets.[12] Call me tainted, but I don't trust that the Land of Lincoln has a clue on how to manage its piggy bank. Based on the state's sullied history of mis-managing finances, I'm betting that the marijuana tax revenue will somehow be diverted or misused down the road, too.

(***Author's note:*** For Illinois, marijuana tax revenue is just another of the myriad failed, magical, silver-bullet tax solutions enacted by its legislators thought to solve Illinois' budget deficits "once and for all." I've come to realize long ago that additional taxes aren't the solution to the deficit problem. Instead, the problem is the folks running Springfield and their inability to allocate scare resources and make the tough choices they are elected to make.)

Worse yet, many of Illinois' revenue streams are from "sin" taxes, which are regressive: disproportionately borne by the poor and minority residents. These *taxes du jour* are voted into legislation by predatory, not benevolent, governments. Red light camera programs, for instance, are disproportionately located in poor and minority neighborhoods under the guise of enhancing public safety. To be clear, red light camera programs are not about safety; they are about *revenue generation*. These programs in Chicago, Illinois, or (*insert your city or state here*), are all about giving a handout to a politician's lobbyist friend who sells red light camera programs. And a kickback (either an overt kickback now, the promise of a lobbyist job, or work the politician's law firm will send his way down the road) will likely be received by your local politician who is supposedly so concerned about the public's safety.

A sheep in wolf's clothing. A trojan horse. And yet the citizenry of Illinois continues to fall for these schemes over and over and over again. Oh, and who has run the great state of Illinois into the ground for the past 100 years, entrenching it as a poster child of the bluest of blue states? Why the great Democrat Party and the voters who continue to elect them. I guess you get the government you deserve. Instead of another sin tax, how about some state programs that bolster manufacturing or services, not more new taxes on everything that some politician thinks are bad: soda, plastic bags, online sports gambling, etc. It's no wonder that its citizens are leaving the state in droves. The paradox is that the state's shrinking populace will be called upon to shoulder more taxes to replace the lost tax revenue from the lost population. This downward death spiral continues until BOOM! The state implodes. And with $134 billion in unfunded pension obligations, Illinois is already at DEFCON 2.

The State of Illinois further backs themselves into a corner and doubles down on the premise that it intends its medical cannabis program only be for "compassionate use" and the medical needs of its residents (and not as a precursor for an adult or recreational use program down the road) when the Act states that *it is prohibited to . . .*

> *. . . Use or possess cannabis if that person does not have a debilitating medical condition and is not a registered qualifying patient or caregiver.*

It sure seems that Illinois' intention is only to have a medical cannabis program. That's it — nothing else. The last time I heard of such reckless doubling down was when I heard the story of the blackjack player who drove to Las Vegas in his $150,000 Mercedes Benz and returned a few days later in a $600,000 Greyhound bus!

So, this is the slippery slope on which most states write their medical cannabis laws. First, make it clear that the enactment of such a medical marijuana act has nothing to do with revenue generation; and second, if not for the pain and suffering of debilitated residents, there would be no need for legalizing cannabis whatsoever. Of course, at a later date, they pull the old switcheroo and shoehorn in the motherlode: a recreational use program.

By the way, props to the bureaucrat who came up with the "Compassionate Care Act," a slick marketing name, better than either Don Draper or Billy Shakespeare could have created. With this branding, the state does not tip its hand that its medical marijuana program is just a way to get its foot in the door with the intention of blowing the door wide open in the future via full adult use legislation.

I think Illinois residents would have a lot more respect for their legislators if these legislators showed a little more respect for their citizens in return. Tell your taxpayers the truth. Tell them up-front that the Compassionate Use

Blah Blah Act is just the first step toward total adult or recreational use of marijuana in the state. Treat us like adults; we're going to find out anyway.

(*Author's note:* In January 2019, a new Democrat governor took office in Illinois [I forget his name, but he's kind of a chubby guy who looks like one of the dudes from Abbot and Costello; some in the media refer to him as Governor *Jelly Belly*]. Soon after that, and notwithstanding all the language in the Compassionate Care Act to the contrary, he announced that Illinois would become a recreational marijuana state effective January 1, 2020. He met that goal, and Illinois became the eleventh state to allow recreational marijuana use.)

But wait. With all the restrictions in the Compassionate Care Act, how can Illinois go recreational? The state has seemingly locked itself into only implementing a medical marijuana program — you know, out of concern for its citizens who suffer from one of a couple of dozen ailments. You just read pertinent parts from the Act itself. *How can this be?*

"Oh, *'it be'.*"

Was Illinois' medical marijuana program and concern for its residents who suffer from chronic disease just a ruse? I guess all of my sarcastic skepticism wasn't misplaced. Shocker!

In this unexpected shift of philosophy (Not!) Illinois' husky governor fella announced three reasons why he pushed the measure to legalize recreational marijuana: a) its criminal justice elements, b) the ability to regulate a product that's already widely available, and c) to bring in revenue. Well, at least Governor *Jelly Belly* came clean on one of the main reasons for this path toward full-on adult use — because it will bring in revenue — much needed revenue to a state which has already been run into the ground by Democrat control for over one hundred years.

(*Author's Note: Dear Springfield, Illinois:* If you're running out of things to tax, how about allowing and taxing online sports betting? How about legalizing and taxing prostitution or those happy ending Asian massage parlors that seem to be popular with NFL team owners these days?)

And lest you think that this is just a revenue grab by the states, think again. Cities have their hands out also. Take the case of the City of Chicago. With an $800 million budget hole to fill for 2020, recently elected Mayor Lori *Leftfoot* (or is it *Lightfoot*? Whatever.) is desperate for revenue of any kind. She inherited the mess which her predecessor, Rahm Emanuel (referred to by many in the media as *Tiny Dancer*), left her, which he, in turn, inherited — the can that got kicked down the road by generations of Chicago Democrat mayors. Her 2020 "Hail Mary" budget includes $3.5 million from recreational marijuana sales and excise taxes in the City of Chicago.[13] (At least this revenue stream is somewhat tangible as compared to her budget's ethereal $538 million from *"savings and efficiencies."*[14] Seems kind of squishy and totally unattainable to me.)

On the other end of the spectrum, many towns are given the ability to opt out of their state's recreational use statutes. In cities like Naperville, IL, a lily-white town with a population of about 150,000 that is routinely ranked in the *Top 10 Best Cities to Raise a Family in America,*[15] the city council has defaulted to a "make no waves," politically correct posture. The soccer mom constituency certainly has an impact on this town. As such, they don't want to sully its carefully crafted family-friendly image. Naperville voted to opt-out of allowing a recreational marijuana dispensary in its confines.

But the states and cities aren't the only entities which are banking on an expansion of "compassionate care" cannabis programs. Methinks the growers and dispensaries in medical marijuana states are already two steps ahead of everybody. They have already prepared for expansion to recreational marijuana based on their product names for this supposed medical marijuana "medicine." (i.e., In my mind, if you need a prescription and a medical marijuana card, then the products being sold are *medicine.* Agree?) However, many cannabis companies' products in medical marijuana states have names that, on the surface, don't seem much like medicinal products. I found *medical* marijuana products with flavors like *Girl Scout Cookies, Key Lime Pie,* and *Animal Cookies.* There are Medical Cannabis Tortilla Chips with flavors such as *Zesty Ranch, Sour Cream & Onion,* and *Salsa Picante.* It doesn't sound much like medicine to me. If these are the names for medical products, I'd sure like my pharmacy to "sexy-up" the boring name of my cholesterol medication and offer various flavor options while they're at it.

JOE CAMEL MARKETING REDUX

When I see advertising on television for mainstream brand name medicines, I don't see too many flavor options. I don't see names that cater more to high schoolers versus the genuinely sick and suffering. I haven't seen marketing targeted at youngsters since *Joe Camel* bit the dust, except in the e-cigarette business circa 2013, when they sold *cotton candy, bubble gum,* and *cookies and cream* flavors, clearly targeted at the youth. And since those early days, the FDA, states, and local government units have been cracking down and sporadically raising the age to purchase e-cigarette products from eighteen to twenty-one years old.

But our so-called medical marijuana states seem to market and target the young (and illegal) end of the spectrum. Shouldn't these "medicines" have Latin or chemical sounding names like my cholesterol medication? If erectile dysfunction medicine followed this practice, then you'd see medicine names like *All Night Long* with slogans like *Guaranteed to make you harder than Chinese arithmetic!*

(**Author's note:** All this slick and deceptive advertising reminds me of a commercial my friend Tony told me about. Tony's a big drinker and one night he's watching TV . . . at home . . . in his underwear, and he comes across a late night commercial: "*. . . if you think you have a drinking problem, then call this number . . .*" Tony looked at the clock [11:30 pm], then at the beer can in his hand, and then at the empty beer cans strewn around the room and thinks he may need help and that this commercial could be for him. He calls the number. To his surprise, it was a liquor store! *Now that's marketing!*)

Imagine if the terrific marketing we see in the cannabis world (as well as the marketing to my friend Tony) expanded to other industries and institutions. For instance, maybe the Catholic Church could get more butts in the pews by offering dipping sauces for communion. Imagine Spicy Avocado,

Ranch, and Teriyaki dipping sauces for communion. That should drive some traffic. Why stop there? Add a selection of blessed energy drinks to add a little jump to your step on Sunday mornings!

(***Continued Author's Note:*** Forgive me, Father, I know not of what I speak.) At the risk of being excommunicated for being sacrilegious, let me go off-topic for a second here to make an additional observation on the Catholic Church. It seems that outsiders view Catholicism as restrictive with too many rules. The following story seems to support that notion:

Catholics intending to get married must attend *Pre-Cana* classes to prepare the couple for marriage in the Catholic Church. Such was the case with three young couples. The priest sat them down at their first Pre-Cana class and reminded them that pre-marital sex violated Catholic Church doctrine, and so to get married in the Catholic Church, they would need to abstain from sex until the class was over, some six-months later.

At the final class, six-months later, the priest asked the couples to report on their vows of abstinence.

The first couple replied, "No problem, Father. We had no sexual urges. Easy-Peasy. Not even any desires. We confirm that we did not have sex." The priest said, "Congratulations, you are welcome to get married in the Catholic Church."

The second couple admitted that they struggled to suppress their sexual urges but explained that they took cold showers to suppress these desires. Like the first couple, they confirmed that they did not have sex. The priest said, "Congratulations, you are welcome to get married in the Catholic Church."

It was now the third couple's turn to give their status. The man told the priest, "I cannot lie, Father. We were doing fairly well until just a few days ago. I happened to see my fiancé bent over, looking into the dryer. Something came over us. We could not control our impulses, and we had wild sex right then and there." The priest said, "I'm sorry. You are no longer welcome in the Catholic Church." The man replied, "I figured as much. We're no longer welcome at the Home Depot, either."

INTERMISSION #2

MAKING PAYROLL

Entrepreneurs who have owned businesses perhaps have one advantage over managers in corporate America who never owned a business: They know what it takes to make payroll. They put their butts on the line with their lenders by making personal guarantees and pledging their assets (often including their own houses). They have "skin in the game," and if they fail, the bank will take their home. Not too many folks in corporate America have their necks on the chopping block if the shit hits the fan in their companies. It is doubtful that these corporate America managers will ever have to tell their significant other that they need to live out of their car for the foreseeable future.

Knowing what it takes to make payroll should be a requirement when running for any local, state, or federal office. For example, look at the recent September 2019 Democrat debate — lots of grandiose ideas regarding healthcare and spending our tax dollars, but no meaningful analysis of how to pay for these largely socialist dreams.

California Senator Kamala Harris, for instance, proposed a $2 trillion (yes *trillion* — I had to review the debate transcripts to be sure) investment in teachers of Historically Black Colleges and Universities (HBCUs):

HARRIS: "*I have, as part of my proposal that we will put $2 trillion into investing in our HBCUs for teachers.*"[16]

Did the good senator mean *billion*? *Million*? Rounding error? In any event, not only did the nine other Democrat contenders not question her on this, I found no questioning or fact-checking that seemed to alarm the national media or general public whatsoever. Was I the only one in America who caught this apparent gaffe?

Not to beat a horse, but as a point of reference consider this: $2 trillion is approximately

- 10% of the national debt, or
- 3.5x the U.S. Department of Defense budget

So, it certainly seems like a misstatement for sure. She is so far off that I can't imagine what she is trying to say. (**Author's note:** In December 2019, the good senator from California announced that she was *suspending* her campaign for President. She cited the inability to properly finance her campaign. Based on her trillion-dollar blunder, it doesn't surprise me. Another thing while I'm at it: why does she say *suspend*? Doesn't she mean she quit or outright gave up? *Suspend* means *to pause*. I'm confused: is she pausing or quitting? Why does she say that she is hitting the pause button when she means she is bowing out of the race altogether? Say what you mean and mean what you say. I'm not a fan of politicians' double-speak.)

Does it matter when the numbers are this large anyway? Aren't these just made-up, imaginary numbers that no one can comprehend? The point is, *are we all so numb to the rhetoric spewing from our public servants and presidential candidates that we don't care if they have a grasp for spending tax dollars?* It's no wonder that our national debt is over $20 trillion: our politicians don't have a clue when it comes to balancing their own presidential campaign checkbooks!

If you're like me, *and I know I am,* then I'd like to see a requirement that, as a prerequisite to running for any public office, candidates must have owned a business at one time or another so that they have practical experience in knowing what it takes to make payroll each week. It will teach them that resources are not unlimited, and must be carefully allocated. My proposed "making payroll" requirement is a real character builder: sleepless nights, learning how to balance budgets (as opposed to gaming the system and just *declaring* a budget is balanced like Lori Leftfoot did), and managing cash flow.

As CFO of several companies, I've sweated out making payroll many times. In the early '90s, I was on the executive team of United Waste Systems, a start-up garbage company located on Fifth Avenue in New York City. We were located on the top floor of a fifty-story building with views of the iconic Plaza Hotel and Central Park. (Some pretty pricey real estate for a garbage company, eh?) I was a newly minted MBA and a young, thirty-one-year-old punk. Our CEO, Bradley Jacobs, was equally young at thirty-five years old.

This was my first gig in raising money and in putting together our Confidential Information Memorandum that told our story and was the basis for accredited investors to, hopefully, throw money at this ground floor opportunity.

Previous to this company, I was a Division Controller at Waste Management. In that role, I didn't know where the money came from to pay bills or make payroll. Those were the CFO's and other executives' problems at corporate headquarters to figure out. I was not responsible for sweating out the cash flow and treasury details. I didn't carry my work home with me. Like a worker at McDonald's who flips his last burger of the week and heads home, I left my work at the office.

As a mid-level manager at Waste Management, my only concern was not if we had cash in the bank to make payroll (again, that was the CFO's job), but rather, "did I enter and *approve* the payroll correctly before the deadline in the company's computer systems?" Similarly, when it came time to replace a $125 thousand garbage truck, I didn't worry if I had enough cash in the bank. Those worries were, again, the responsibility of the company's CFO and bankers at huge financial institutions. Instead, my only concern was, "did I complete the Capital Expenditure Request form correctly so the shiny new truck would show up at our facility on-time as budgeted?"

At United Waste, however, the responsibilities of having cash in the bank to make payroll and pay bills fell squarely on my shoulders. Now *I* was responsible for making payroll and making sure we had our banking and investor relations buttoned up. Companies seemingly never have enough cash. Cash is a scarce resource and needs to be managed and prioritized carefully. Many politicians and entrepreneurs do not understand this.

We never had enough cash to do all the things we wanted to. (What start-up does?) We were running low on dough in the summer of 1991, and I had to alert Bradley. "Brad," I started, "I have good news and bad news." A curious, Woody Allen-looking Brad asked, "What's the good news, Dean?" I responded, "I found enough money to last us until tomorrow." Naturally, like a set-up in an Abbot and Costello routine, he then asked, "What's the bad news?" I stoically answered, "I meant to tell you yesterday!" Brad said, "No way." "*Way,*" I replied. Without missing a beat, Brad responded, "Well, I guess we better hustle up some more dough."

And, he did. Brad called on his investors, and within a few days, we had another $1 million to put in the gas tank. Yadda, yadda . . . and one year later, after a dozen or so carefully executed and integrated acquisitions, United Waste Systems went public on NASDAQ. Within the next six years, the company completed close to one hundred successful acquisitions and then sold to USA Waste for $2 billion. $2 billion! And I was there when we couldn't even make payroll!

(***Author's note:*** Bradley Jacobs was just getting started. He went on to found United Rentals, the largest equipment rental company in the world, by rolling-up the mom-and-pop equipment rental industry. He followed that up by growing freight logistics provider XPO Logistics from about $40 million in revenue to about $18 billion in close to ten years. Like Wayne Huizenga, Bradley is a world-class entrepreneur. I consider myself lucky to have worked for both.)

DIRTY LITTLE SECRET #3

INVESTORS BEWARE: ACCOUNTING SCANDALS AND WASTED RESOURCES!

You may think that the folks running today's cannabis companies understand the need for consistent, transparent, and accurate financial reporting that reflects the financial health of the company, and that audited financials should give comfort to cannabis industry investors. You may think that the companies staff themselves with qualified accounting professionals and have basic internal controls in place. You may think that shareholder capital is invested carefully. Think again.

The predominant accounting software used in the nascent cannabis industry is *QuickBooks,* which is ill-suited for the financial reporting and consolidation needs of more than one entity, let alone forty, fifty (or more) entities. And so, the accounting task with forty or more legal entities quickly becomes a nightmare, especially if the understaffed accounting department lacks experienced professionals, and uses accounting software designed for single-entity donut shops — not a multi-state business with dozens of legal entities.

Most pot companies in the industry have unsophisticated mom-and-pop owners. They scraped together the several hundred thousands of dollars needed to complete a dispensary license application in their state. Then, the lucky winners of licenses face cobbling together the necessary capital to get their stores up and running. State application fees and annual license fees can range from $5 thousand to $100 thousand; the buildout of the dispensary can run $250 thousand to $1 million; and the working capital (needed for inventory, payroll, etc. before the business starts cash flowing) can be another $500 thousand. Building out cultivation centers will set them back $10 - $15 million — serious dough.

Publicly-traded companies on the U.S. and other worldwide stock exchanges are heavily regulated. In the U.S., the Securities and Exchange Commission (SEC) sets forth rules specifying, among other things, audit requirements (including a review of the entity's internal controls), that financial statements be presented following Generally Accepted Accounting Principles (GAAP), and the required content to be discussed in the Management Discussion and Analysis (MDA) of quarterly and annual results.

All financial statements need to speak the same language. In the U.S., that language is GAAP. The rest of the world uses International Financial Reporting Standards or IFRS. The U.S. is moving toward IFRS, but the point is that the investors need to know that the companies they invest in speak the same financial language so that financial statements have integrity and can be relied on and compared across companies.

Such is the case in the cannabis industry: investors need some assurance that the financial statements as presented are comparable to others in the industry. *Dirty Little Secret #3* is that the cannabis industry suffers from a lack of reliable, consistent, and timely financial reporting and that these companies waste an inordinate amount of shareholders' invested funds along the way. The founders of Cannabis 2.0 companies are not accountants, don't know what accountants do, and in general, are not knowledgeable about GAAP, IFRS, or audits. In their previous lives, maybe in running a small privately-held company, their financial statements may have been prepared on a cash-basis and perhaps for the sole purpose of filing their annual tax return. But cash-basis financial statements are materially different than GAAP financial statements, which are commonly required in companies that raise money and have many shareholders. Most Cannabis 2.0 entrepreneurs don't know this, of course, because *they don't know what they don't know*. Further exacerbating financial statement reliability is that these cannabis company founders have tended to under-invest in back office functions like accounting, financial reporting, financial planning and analysis, human resources, and other administrative functions. Their companies simply may not be capable of producing GAAP financial statements.

RAMPANT ACCOUNTING SCANDALS: INVESTORS BEWARE

Already in Cannabis 2.0, there have been many blockbuster accounting and compliance scandals. Arguably, taking the cake in Cannabis 2.0 scandals is the July 2019 revelation that CannTrust, a publicly-held cannabis company, admitted that its CEO and other C-level officers knew of growing unlicensed marijuana crops. This nefarious action caused Health Canada to put all of CannTrust's sales on hold. CannTrust's stock dropped 57% in July alone. With this chum in the water, the sharks circled, and several class-action law-suits were filed against CannTrust. In August, KPMG, CannTrust's audi-tors withdrew several of its audits for 2018 and its March 2019 quarter. By December 2019, its stock was trading at *just 8%* of its all-time high in March 2019. Where was CannTrust's compliance function? Where was its Board of Directors?

By November 2019, many other high-profile securities lawsuits had been filed against Cannabis 2.0 companies including, Aurora Cannabis, Inc; Canopy Growth; CuraLeaf Holdings, Inc.; Liberty Health Sciences, Inc; 22nd Century Group, Sundial Growers, and more.[17] You can bet these won't be the only compliance and accounting scandals rooted in Cannabis 2.0. These lawsuits underscore the lack of internal controls and Board oversight that are rampant in the cannabis industry, which provides fertile soil for other scan-dals and shareholder lawsuits.

With Cannabis 2.0 companies' management lacking in experience and integrity, and the companies themselves lacking internal controls and the ability to produce even the most basic financial information, one must wonder if the cannabis industry is even *investment grade*. Do you want to risk *your* money with Cannabis 2.0 companies at this time?

COMPANY E: "IT'S TAX TIME . . . WHERE'S MY FRICKIN' K-1?"

In addition to numerous Cannabis 2.0 accounting scandals, the lack of experience in investor relations by Cannabis 2.0 management teams have caused problems for Cannabis 2.0 investors as well. Because most cannabis companies are legally established as LLCs, they do not file taxes. Instead, an LLC's profits and losses are the responsibility of the investors. LLC's will issue Schedule K-1s to investors at tax time, which will detail their share of the company's profits or losses they need to include on their individual tax returns. These K-1s are required before individuals can file their tax returns, and getting them on time can be like pulling teeth.

In an imaginary world, LLCs are buttoned up and file their U.S. Federal (IRS) tax returns by March 15 and send K-1s to their individual investors so that they will be able to include them with and file their own tax returns by the customary April 15 due date. But this is just theory, nirvana, like unicorns and rainbows. Because of poor financial infrastructure and internal controls in start-up companies, year-end tax time tends to be a fire drill for both the companies and the investors. Because they don't have all relevant information, LLCs almost always file extensions to submit their tax returns. Instead of filing their final tax return by March 15, an extension allows them to file by September 15.

Companies that file extensions usually means that its investors will also need to file an extension because they can't file their final individual tax return until the company files its final return and issues a *final* K-1 to the investor. It is customary that companies filing extensions will provide *estimated K-1s* to their investors by early April, allowing investors a few weeks to determine if they will, likewise, need to file extensions with the IRS before their April 15 deadline.

In January 2019, Susan, Company E's experienced CFO, was trying to avoid a tax season fire drill. She advised Chad, Company E's founder, to be proactive, and as a courtesy to the company's shareholders, she was going to send a letter to shareholders providing year end tax planning and timing information. The communication was to go to all shareholders by the end of January and would advise that the company would be filing an extension and that shareholders should expect to receive estimated K-1s by April 1 so that they could plan accordingly.

Of course, the need for this type of communication to shareholders wasn't on Chad's radar screen. Ever the marketer, he thought this tax communication was an opportune vehicle to also update shareholders on the results of operations for the previous calendar year and then gloat about the prospects for the upcoming year.

Good idea but bad execution. It took over two months for Company E's communication department to pin Chad down and put this simple communication together, effectively holding the originally intended shareholder communication regarding important and time-sensitive tax issues hostage. Of course, Susan saw this coming. Despite her best efforts in being proactive, the young founder screwed-up the plan. Fast forward a couple of months to March 2019: still, no communication went out to the shareholders, and Susan's phone is ringing off the hook with frantic investors (or their CPA designates) wondering:

- when will they receive their estimated K-1s;
- if the company had positive net income, and, if so:
    * what is the estimate of their share of the company's income they will need to report on their tax returns? and
    * when would the company make a distribution to them, and in what amount to enable them to pay for their tax liability stemming from their investment in the company?

In the case where the company is profitable, investors expect that the company provide distributions (i.e., cash) to the shareholders to cover their tax obligation from their investment.

Again, this is how it is *supposed* to work. But for many fledgling Cannabis 2.0 companies led by inexperienced owners who skimp on back-office functions like accounting, financial reporting, and tax advice, they don't have a clue. That said, as an investor in privately-held cannabis companies, you must prepare for several potential surprises.

Surprise #1 is even if your Shareholder Agreement specifies the right to receive quarterly and annual financial statements, don't count on the digit-heads in accounting or even the company owners being aware of this obligation. More often than not, you can bet that they won't automatically be sent to you on time, if at all — plan on needing time to request these statements from the company. Also, expect them not to be accurate if and when you do receive them.

Surprise #2 is when companies don't provide year-end tax calendar guidance (including when estimated K-1s will be available). Don't expect inexperienced owners who have never worked in corporate environments before to be aware of critical, customary tax and investor-related protocols. Unless the company's CFO or tax professionals are on top of things, don't expect them to put your needs at the top of their priority list. Remember, these companies operate in the world of Hooterville.

Surprise #3 is when the company is profitable but hasn't managed its cash flow to provide shareholders the cash distributions necessary to pay their tax obligations stemming from their investment. Surprise #3 is undoubtedly the most problematic of all the surprises because when a company is profitable, investors will most likely incur a tax obligation from their share of the company's profits allocated to them, as stipulated by their K-1. Regardless of whether or not the company made a distribution to shareholders (as is customary in this situation), paying these taxes is ultimately the sole obligation of the investor, not the company.

Before investing in privately-held cannabis companies, ask yourself:

- "Does the management team of the cannabis company I invested in (or am thinking of investing in) and its third-party tax and legal professionals have experience and competence to effectively and professionally manage through these IRS reporting requirements and consequences?"

- "Are they proactive and ahead of the game, or are they always playing catch up?" (Don't assume they have even the most basic investor relations tools like always having an up-to-date e-mail contact list for shareholders.)

- "Do they treat my sensitive data with encryption or use secure portals?" (Typically, correspondence containing sensitive investment and tax documents that contain social security, birthdate, name/address, and other confidential information should be transmitted via secure means and should not flow through unsecure e-mail channels ready for hacking by nefarious actors from around the globe. You don't want your personal information and e-mails to be confiscated like Hillary's were from her personal server that she kept in the bathroom. *Russia, are you listening?*)

- "Will I get regular communication and updates regarding financial statements and ETAs for K-1s or, instead, will I or my CPA need to constantly lob calls into the company and pull information from them?"

COMPANY *F:* A VERY LIBERAL VACATION POLICY

Management is responsible for preparing a company's financial statements in accordance with GAAP, so they fairly present the results of operations and the financial health of the company. When audited, there should be minimal adjustments by the auditors.

Year-end audit adjustments are kept to a minimum when a company has robust internal controls, seasoned accounting professionals, and an experienced Board of Directors with an audit committee that understands its fiduciary responsibility to shareholders. Many controllers have lost their jobs because the auditors suggested just one or two audit adjustments during the annual audit. After all, too many or material year-end audit adjustments render the company's interim financial statements, which are relied on throughout the year, useless.

As a by-product of management not having experience in public companies, Cannabis 2.0 companies have typically under-invested in their accounting, human resource, and administrative functions. As such, these companies lack sound processes, internal controls, qualified personnel, and an experienced Board. In this undisciplined environment, investors and others must use caution when using company-prepared financial statements, whether audited or not.

Many Cannabis 2.0 companies do not follow basic Accounting 101 processes: they don't reconcile bank accounts, properly prepare consolidated statements, formulate the accrual of annual bonuses, include all accounts payable invoices in the financial statements (because they are sitting on somebody's desk), and on and on and on. In most Cannabis 2.0 companies, the back-office processes and functions, including the accounting function, take a back seat to marketing, operations, and even mergers and acquisitions. Because a solid foundation of processes and internal controls does not exist, acquisitions are piled upon an already shaky foundation, further exacerbating the financial reporting problems.

My favorite example of how a lack of internal controls affects the accuracy of the financial statements occurred at Company F. A very inexperienced bookkeeper, Donna, was hired by Dave, Company F's CEO, to prepare the financial statements at its cultivation center. Donna had no experience in closing books. The concept of accruing for property taxes, insurance, and payroll was foreign to her. She was closing the books monthly on a cash-basis and not an accrual basis as required by Generally Accepted Accounting Principles, Company F's Shareholder Agreements, and, in general, by most of world outside of Hooterville.

The auditors found it unusual that Donna's financial statements did not reflect a liability for unused vacation time, as is typical in financial statements prepared according to GAAP. Of course, Donna didn't know any better, and Dave was clueless. At audit time, Donna reviewed how she administered Company F's vacation policy with the audit partner. She explained, "In the first year you get two weeks, in the second year you get four weeks, and in the third year and beyond, you get eight weeks of vacation."

Eight weeks? Really? Where do I sign up? Even the State of Illinois and the Chicago Teachers Union employees don't have it this good. Many companies don't even offer four weeks' vacation; and, those that do usually require over ten years' service. Any experienced worker would know that eight weeks' vacation is unheard of after three years. But not to Donna. She is underqualified and has never prepared a GAAP financial statement before. She doesn't know any better.

It gets worse. The methodology used by Donna in tracking and administering Company F's vacation policy allowed employees to forego actually taking vacation time (after all, after the fifth or sixth week of vacation the employees are probably running out of places to jet off to), and instead, opt to receive payment in cash for their unused vacation time. It wasn't unusual to see the weekly payroll include payments for $4,000 or more to certain employees who cashed out their unused vacation time. That's how Donna ran the program. Having no relevant accounting experience in preparing accurate financial statements, this all seemed reasonable to her. Meanwhile, the employees most probably knew they were the beneficiaries of Donna's foolishness to the tune of hundreds of thousands of dollars over the past three years.

All the while, Dave never reviewed the weekly payroll, which is a necessary internal control procedure at non-Hootervillian companies. Dave thought that the vacation policy that he told Donna to administer was "no vacation in the first year and only one week of vacation after one year and each year following that." Pretty stingy. Just one week no matter how long you've been with the company. Quite the delta between how Dave thought the vacation policy was being administered and how Donna was actually administering the policy. Donna was Santa Claus, and Dave was Scrooge.

Worse yet, Company F's Employee Handbook contradicted both Donna and Dave. The two-paragraph Vacation Policy section referred the reader to "the attached Vacation Schedule." Guess what? Nowhere in the *ninety*-page Employee Handbook did this Vacation Schedule exist. With three different versions of a vacation policy floating around, the audit partner was beside herself. She asked, "How could this be? What are employees told when they are hired? You mean to tell me that not one of over one hundred employees hired since the cultivation center opened its doors asked to see the missing Vacation Schedule even though they are required to acknowledge receiving the Employee Handbook?" Only in Hooterville.

The audit partner reviewed her findings with Dave, and he went ballistic. How can Donna be running this charity program right under his nose, and he wasn't aware? Dave estimated that Donna had paid Company F's employees hundreds of thousands of dollars more than his version of the policy would have yielded. Apparently, the administration of company policies wasn't a big concern for Dave; after all, like the rest of Cannabis 2.0 executives, he was preoccupied in bidding wars for cannabis companies at ridiculous prices. All told, Company F had about $100,000 of vacation liability in the current year that wasn't on the books. The entry would require that the financials be restated and show $100,000 less profitability.

Worse yet, going forward, the company had to right this wrong with its employees. The party was over. This was a no-win human resource issue. Taking benefits away from employees usually is.

When the dust settled on Company F's audit, there weren't only one or two audit adjustments: the audit generated *more than fifty* audit adjustments reflecting Dave's neglect and lack of investment in and understanding of the importance of the accounting function over the past several years. The total of these audit adjustments caused a reduction in reported profits by about $4 million. Whoopsie daisy. The pre-audit financial statements which the company prepared and were previously and liberally distributed by Dave to investors, regulators, and used in state license applications were materially incorrect. The unaudited financials painted a picture of a much healthier company than was the case. As it turned out, the financial statements that investors received and then relied on to negotiate the terms of an investment and determine whether or not to make the investment were not worth the paper they were written on. It sounds like a lawsuit waiting to happen! (**Author's note:** If Company F was running low on toilet paper, they could have utilized their pre-audited financial statements instead.)

This is just one example of shoddy bookkeeping as a result of under-investment in the back office and symptomatic of what is happening in Cannabis 2.0 companies and why their financial statements, even if audited and available, should be used with caution.

Company G: Ready, Fire, Aim!

I once worked for a successful entrepreneur who used the metaphor of "taking time to sharpen the saw." Meaning: if you are always busy sawing, your saw blade will become dull. Fools continue to saw wood, thinking that just doing something is better than doing nothing. The wisest lumberjacks, however, know that taking time out from the act of sawing to sharpen the blade, even though there is no sawing taking place in the ten minutes it takes to sharpen the blade, will achieve the best results in the long run.

A lot of companies and entrepreneurs fall victim to the fallacy that you need to *keep busy being busy* and keep *doing stuff,* so they don't take time to analyze and plan. They don't hold meetings to keep everyone on the same page. They don't invest in training for their employees and managers. They never sharpen the saw. Companies like this don't have regularly scheduled meetings to keep everyone rowing in the same direction. Everything is done by the seat-of-their pants. Everyone is putting out fires. In this environment, companies are wildly chaotic, inefficient, and not well-oiled machines. Without processes, competent and experienced managers are exponentially more *inefficient* and spend a lot of time and money fixing mistakes from their haste. Haste makes waste? You bet.

Having won a license to build a grow/cultivation center in an Eastern state, Company G's CEO, Carmen, was in such a hurry to start construction

that he immediately purchased the structural components for a pre-fabri-
cated indoor cultivation facility and had them delivered to the site so that
the construction company could begin assembling a permanent indoor grow
facility. Never mind that the state license clearly stipulated that a greenhouse,
and not a permanent indoor facility, be built. This first tranche of pre-fab
building materials that Carmen ordered cost about $500 thousand. And so,
construction of a permanent indoor grow facility began with Carmen thinking all the while that the state would prefer a permanent grow facility over a
greenhouse any day. When the state inspectors found that Company G was
building a permanent building instead of the approved greenhouse, it noti-
fied Company G that it would pull the license.

Carmen was bewildered. In his mind, the state should view his construction of a permanent indoor grow facility in place of a greenhouse as
his going above and beyond. In his mind, he should be getting a pat on the
back instead of having his license threatened. When Carmen finally realized
that the state couldn't take a joke anymore and was serious that Company G
adhere to the stipulations of the license (i.e. that it build a greenhouse and
not a permanent indoor grow facility), it was too late to return the pre-fab
building materials to the supplier.

Carmen had to return the first parcel of land he purchased for the
permanent building to its original condition, which required the builders
to remove the foundations they poured at the cost of almost $100 thou-
sand. Then, he had to hire an architect to re-work the drawings to build the
greenhouse that met with the state's specifications. Since he could not return
the pre-fab building components, he instructed the architects to incorpo-
rate these components in the new greenhouse design somehow so the money
spent was not totally wasted. In so doing, however, it created a wholly inefficient and undesirable design.

So, what did it cost Carmen and Company G by not sharpening the
saw? It cost an extra $100 thousand in site development costs to return the
false start to its original condition. Additionally, Carmen incurred $500 thou-
sand in building components that he wouldn't have needed had he followed

the state's specs and built a greenhouse. Finally, and most costly, Carmen forever saddled Company G's operations with an utterly inefficient design that will cost untold millions of dollars in inefficiencies over the life of the facility. When you don't measure twice and cut once, yes, haste makes waste.

COMPANY H: A $100,000 MONTHLY LEASE?

In another blunder caused by "just doing it," let's look at Company H, which had recently purchased a license in Florida.

Licenses in Florida are vertically integrated. One license allows for one cultivation center, which grows the weed to sell through its network of up to thirty dispensaries. As soon as the company purchased the license and under some time pressure (per state regulations) to open the first store by a specified date, Company H's management team descended upon Florida to begin identifying cities and properties to site its dispensaries. The young team was similar to Company C's management team in that it was enthralled with "shiny objects." So, it was natural that they *had* to be in Miami's South Beach. (I guess to be close to Pit Bull?) The team identified "the best" property on which they would build the "flagship" store for the entire company. Never mind the minutiae of a lease. That's just paperwork to be worked out later.

Edward, Company H's owner, negotiated the lease for what would be the company's flagship store, or so he thought. In Edward's mind, he negotiated to sublease 4,000 square feet of the 10,000 square foot retail location. In his haste, Edward and the landlord entered into a handshake deal. (*A handshake? What could possibly go wrong?*) The lease for the entire building would run $100 thousand per month! Yes, only $1.2 million per year. If I didn't know any better, I would have thought that Senator Kamala Harris negotiated this lease.

A bit of perspective: Company H also owned a great little dispensary in California. This small, eight hundred square foot store did over $6 million of revenue per year (probably in the top decile of revenue for dispensaries in the country; close to rivaling the revenue per square foot of Apple stores), and the rent was only $72,000 per year! That's only $6,000 per month! That store is a money maker with a favorable combination of low rent and lots of top-line revenue. It seems like a formula for success to me, flagship store, or not!

Soon, Mary Ann, Company H's CFO, began getting monthly invoices from the South Beach property's landlord. The invoice was for the full $100,000, not the 40% purported sublet amount that Edward had thought he and the landlord verbally agreed to. Mary Ann asked Edward to see the lease so she could determine if the invoice was commensurate with the terms Edward negotiated. She thought, *"Surely, all the details are codified in the lease."* In Edward's haste to stake his claim in South Beach, the lease was, in his mind, a mere formality that would follow the handshake. (When Edward ran a private company, he never worried about such trivialities.)

Surprise! The company had not drawn up a lease. With only a handshake, Company H and its shareholders were now in the unfortunate position where it would need to rely on the landlord's good character and memory, both of which are in short supply in the cannabis industry.

The landlord didn't remember the deal the way Edward did. (Shocker!) Instead of Company H being the *sublessor* for 40% of the space, the landlord recalled the agreement was Company H was the lessor, responsible for 100% of the space. Further, the landlord recalled that Edward agreed to take 70% of the space and that he would allow Edward to sublet the other 3,000 square feet. A case of "*he* said, *he* said" reminiscent of similar cases found on *The People's Court.* So now Edward and the landlord had to square the circle. In the absence of a written lease, something that is considered requisite in nearly every industry except, apparently, in Cannabis 2.0, Edward had just exposed Company H (and its shareholders) to the whims of the landlord's recollection. Sloppy.

Because of a lack of internal controls, processes, and Edward's inexperience in the protocols of running a company with shareholders, he put the company in a position in which it should not be. So, now playing defense, he had to re-negotiate what he thought was already negotiated. Edward capitulated and caved to the landlord's demands. Edward had been played.

The deal that he finally agreed to was that Company H would take 60% of the space and sublet the other 40% to the landlord's wife's yoga studio. Really? A yoga studio? I don't know how many yoga studios can afford a $2,000 per month lease, let alone *$40,000 per month*. And, remember, being the lessor, Company H (and its shareholders) will be stuck holding the bag when the yoga studio can't pay its rent. Talk about a downward dog! I think Company H is getting screwed doggy style on this one.

It gets worse. Mary Ann found out that it would take a year before the proper licenses would be effective in Miami for this dispensary. This meant that Company H would be paying $100,000 in monthly rent (while trying to collect on another $40,000 from the yoga studio) for a full year without generating a dime of revenue. Did Edward include this in the financial calculus when he chose this South Beach location for its flagship store? Oh, never mind. *Just do it* — remember?

It gets worse again. The so-called flagship store would require an elaborate build-out. Usually, a build-out for a dispensary would cost $250 - $500 thousand. But for this, the *flagship* store, no expenses would be spared, so plan on $1 million.

Well, Mary Ann thought, "at least it's the *flagship* store; surely revenues would be huge." So, she looked at Edward's projections for this flagship store, expecting to see annual revenue projections in the $15 million range. Not the case. In the words of *Scooby-Doo,* "*Rut roh.*"[18] Not only were the revenues not commensurate with the rent, but they also weren't on par with the little "cash register" of a dispensary that Company H owned in Los Angeles. The revenue projections for the company's South Beach flagship store were only $3.5 million in the next full year!

And these are the types of owners/managers that litter the cannabis industry landscape. They are inexperienced kids who are spending investors' hard-earned cash: kids chasing shiny objects with no experience in running complex companies. This is bush-league stuff, amateur hour. Unfortunately, it is typical of the management commonly found in the cannabis industry circa 2018-2019. Many Cannabis 2.0 companies went on acquisition spending sprees at ridiculous prices. These companies' strategy was to build critical mass and sell the overvalued mess to some other sucker, usually an already public company needing to show growth. The crash in cannabis stock valuations in the second half of 2019 reflects the folly and unsustainability of this flawed strategy.

The good news is that as Cannabis 3.0 emerges from the Cannabis 2.0 ashes, these rookie management teams will be squeezed out, marginalized, and replaced by competent management. Hopefully, chaos, lack of corporate governance, seat-of-the-pants decisions, and sloppy or non-existent documentation will be in short supply in Cannabis 3.0.

COMPANY I: I THOUGHT WE WERE GOING PUBLIC

In mid-2018, many cannabis companies started out on a trajectory to go public but shifted gears midstream. Yeppers, "going public" sounds neat, trendy, and is a badge of honor. The problem is that inexperienced owners that run these cannabis companies don't have a clue. Once these inexperienced owners figured out that being public meant they could no longer run their companies in the same manner that they were accustomed to, they shifted gears to an easier, more immediate, but less lucrative path to monetize their companies: a sale to an already public company.

From mid-2018 through 2019 Q1, during a period which can only be described as hyper-frenzied cannabis industry consolidation, most anyone with a cannabis license, usually a single grow facility or dispensary, had, no doubt, received many offers to be purchased. Many of these offers were unsolicited and from publicly and privately-held MSOs, which were desperate to show continued growth to keep their hamster wheels turning. As such, these MSOs knocked on every door they could to entice mom-and-pops to sell their licenses and companies for a little cash and a lot of stock (as it turned out — a lot of *overvalued* stock). Company I was one such company that was "in play," meaning that it entered into a Letter of Intent to be purchased by another larger company. As is customary, only a handful of employees at Company I were "in the know," or as one executive liked to say, "under the tent." The reason for this secrecy was to minimize disruption to the company and its employees who would otherwise be distracted if they knew their employer had hung out the "For Sale" shingle.

The typical acquisition process should work as follows: The Acquiring Company makes an offer to purchase the Selling Company. If the Selling Company is interested, it negotiates a non-binding Letter of Intent with the Acquiring Company. The Acquiring Company assembles a team comprised of management, attorneys, accountants, and tax counsel to conduct due diligence on the Selling Company; a Due Diligence Item Request list is prepared for the Selling Company team to complete. They upload the requested documents into a cloud-based secure data room; the Acquiring Company's attorneys review and follow up on requests and this process is rinsed and repeated a few more times until the Acquiring Company is satisfied it understands the economics, prospects, and risks associated with purchasing the Selling Company. A Definitive Purchase Agreement is entered into by both parties and a closing date is set.

The main reason that Company I threw in the towel and decided not to go public was, like other companies, it previously didn't properly invest in its back office. They were never able to dig themselves out of the hole caused by years of under-investment despite over $1 million spent on accountants to try to get its books in order for an RTO. In the end, Company I's owners decided that selling to a competitor rather than going public themselves was the easiest and fastest path to monetizing their investment. As they started down the going public process, they realized that they didn't have a clue as to what would be involved in running a public company. After several months of dealing with auditors, lawyers, and the like, they didn't like what they saw in terms of the discipline that being a public company would require from them. They were in over their heads. *They didn't know what they didn't know.* In deciding to sell their company rather than go public, they left hundreds of millions of dollars on the table for their investors who didn't have a say in the matter.

INTERMISSION #3

THE IMMACULATE CONCEPTION

How did the universe start? How did life on earth begin? Where do babies come from? These are some mind-boggling mega-questions. It hurts my head to contemplate these weighty issues. Kind of like Larry and his professor pondering that *"our entire solar system could be, like one tiny atom in the fingernail of some other giant being"* while smoking some marijuana in *Animal House*.[19] Pretty heady stuff. My head is about to explode.

Well, the cannabis industry has a doozy of its own: *Where do license holders get the initial supply of marijuana for their grow facilities when it wins a state cultivation license?*

We all know that marijuana is federally illegal, and the states legislate their own marijuana laws. Further, it is unlawful to transport marijuana across state lines. So how, then, does a state-legislated marijuana program start? Where do the seeds come from? Certainly, they can't cross state lines, can they?

The various state cannabis acts are relatively silent on the genesis issue of the initial planting at a licensed cultivation facility. You know, *don't ask, don't tell,* just start growing the MJ while the state looks the other way. The truth is that the states don't want to know. Most of them mandate only that facilities turn on their security cameras (which are required inside every grow facility and are monitored by the state's regulatory personnel) right before the first harvest occurs. Effectively, they don't want to see how the sausage is made. They activate the cameras only after Santa Claus brings the bounty of cannabis plants in the dark of night.

This paradox is, appropriately, called the *Immaculate Conception.*

DIRTY LITTLE SECRET #4

MANY CANNABIS INDUSTRY 2.0 C-SUITE OCCUPANTS LACK EXPERIENCE, INTEGRITY, AND ARE ETHICALLY CHALLENGED

Give me your tired, your poor,
Your huddled masses, yearning to breathe free,
The wretched refuse of your teeming shore,
Send these, the homeless, tempest tost to me,
I lift my lamp beside the golden door.[20]

Inscription, Statue of Liberty, circa 1903

Give me your dreamers, your entrepreneurs
who have won cannabis licenses,
Your inexperienced billionaire wannabes yearning to make millions,
The wretched refuse of other industries,
Send these, the inept, opportunistic and greedy to me,
I offer a once-in-a-lifetime opportunity . . . but you need to act fast!

Cannabis industry, circa 2018

It is easy to succumb to the belief that someone that has been granted a cannabis cultivation, processing/manufacturing, distribution, or dispensary (retail) license by a state must know what they are doing. After all, they seem to have anointed themselves as *de facto* experts in this fledgling industry.

Not quite. Hacks, hucksters and carnival barkers lacking relevant experience in scaling and managing large corporate enterprises fill the industry.

I want to be clear: I'm not disparaging Cannabis 2.0 entrepreneurs. Most are resourceful, have a tireless work ethic, and all that. They put an entire industry on the map. Kudos and congrats. I am merely saying that, in general, they don't have the skills needed to scale their companies and take them to the proverbial next level. Some cannabis execs readily admit this; however, many believe their own hype.

Perhaps I've been spoiled, having worked in both start-ups as well as for a few world-class entrepreneurs in a variety of industries. Seeing the forest from the trees, and without going into detail, let's just say that there is a significant talent gap between those at the helm of Cannabis 2.0 companies (from its smallest, privately-held companies to its largest publicly-held companies) and the rest of the world's industries. As with other consolidating industries, truly experienced talent with relevant experience will replace these Wild West pioneers in the coming years.

Remember that in the incipiency of the cannabis industry, these licenses were won not by seasoned corporate entities, but instead, by mom-and-pops. With dry cleaner operators, restauranteurs, middle-level managers of mid-size companies, and the like having won licenses granted by the various states, one must remember that while there is a lot of ambition and sweat equity demonstrated by these pioneers, that most of them don't have the chops or experience to be successful in a consolidating industry, let alone the skills necessary to transform their cannabis company into a highly-valued Multi-State Operator.

Perhaps their biggest weakness is *they don't know what they don't know.*

MedMen's fall from grace

Keep in mind that I'm just the messenger here. Meet Adam Bierman and Andrew Modlin, who are at the helm at MedMen, the iconic Cannabis 2.0 retailer based out of California. It was once a unicorn with a billion-dollar valuation. Their qualifications to run a billion-dollar company? Reportedly, Adam was a sports agent representing minor league baseball players, and Andrew was a painter turned brand designer. They also reportedly ran a marketing company together. Bierman famously bragged in April 2019 to *Rolling Stone* magazine: "There is no reason we cannot be the biggest marijuana company on the planet. I'm sitting with aces in the game of a lifetime. I'm not slowing down."[21] In a January 2017 interview, Modlin stated, "I think what sets us apart is a seamless integration of capital and operational expertise."[22] Hmmm. With this amount of hubris and arrogance, and with no relevant experience, what could go wrong here?

After a year of self-aggrandizement, on November 15, 2019, a Friday afternoon — a favorite time for companies (and politicians) to release bad news — MedMen announced massive layoffs and a "plan to achieve positive EBITDA."[23] I guess after a year of freefall in which Medmen's OTCQX-listed stock lost almost 90% of its value from October 2018 that either MedMen's Chairman couldn't take a joke anymore or Adam and Andrew, self-proclaimed cannabis industry visionaries, found religion in a last-ditch effort to keep their jobs, save face, and try to save the company. How long did they think they could continue to burn through investors' cash (and CFOs)?

(***Author's note:*** For a good chuckle, I encourage you to read the press release for yourself. For an even greater laugh, read some news articles featuring MedMen's co-founders from 2018 and compare their prognostications at that time to the state of the industry and their company as of 2019 Q4, only a year later. While they sound visionary in these 2018 articles, as it is playing out, these thirty-somethings had a lot of people fooled, including themselves.)

Here are some excerpts from MedMen's November 15, 2019 press release which seems obvious to non-cannabis experienced executives, but is apparently late-breaking news for the two thirty-somethings running MedMen:

- MedMen announced a "strategic plan to achieve its target of positive EBITDA by the end of the calendar year 2020."
  - * *Goal-setting, a novel idea. It seems that achieving positive EBITDA should have been a goal all along, and it appears that they just bought themselves another year to achieve it. My bet is that MedMen will miss this deadline as long as Adam and Andrew remain at the helm.*
- "MedMen will be providing layoff notices to 190 employees, including 80 corporate employees."
  - * *What the hell were all these people doing on the payroll anyway?*
  - * *Are these people losing their jobs so that Adam and Andrew can continue to pay themselves outlandish salaries and perquisites?*
- "We must unlock our operating leverage and bring the Company to positive EBITDA. Given market conditions, capital allocation is more critical than ever."
  - * *Duh! Capital allocation is always critical, so is reducing cash burn. Glad they finally figured this out. Welcome to the real-world.*
- MedMen says it will "Monetize Minority Investments," "Scale Delivery Platforms," and "Re-align Performance Incentives."
  - * *It looks as if they have already checked out the Bullshit Generator website! (See Intermission #7.)*
- MedMen will reduce corporate sales and general and administrative (SG&A) expenses from a run rate of $154 million (December 2018) to $85 million by the end of 2020 Q3.
  - * *Who's minding the store? How do they have a $154 million run rate for SG&A expenses when their revenue run rate is only $160 million? Let me guess: "Because it's a land grab?"*
  - * *How much of that $154 million run rate SG&A is attributed to Adam's and Andrew's reported extravagant spending*

— including $3 million in salaries, millions in bonuses, twenty-four-hour armed Executive Protection, high-tech safe rooms and security systems for your houses, personal drivers, private jets (often with friends and family along for the ride), special-order pearl white Escalades for Adam, and another for a family member's custom $160,000 Tesla, and placing Adam's personal therapist and marriage counselor on staff fulltime at a rate of $300,000 a year?[24]

The press release seems to be in reaction to a realization that this management team better get its shit together — and fast! Maybe, just maybe, Adam didn't have "the aces in the game of a lifetime" after all. And maybe Andrew was wrong when he said, "I think what sets us apart is a seamless integration of capital and operational expertise."

Their *mea culpa* press release smacks of a guy who gets a DUI and tells his wife: "I'm sorry. I'm never going to drink again. I'll come straight home after work. I'll go to counseling and church and Alcoholics Anonymous." Blah, blah, blah. The problem is, one month later, this guy will be drinking again and forget about his day of atonement. I'm not betting that MedMen will achieve its goal to be EBITDA positive by 2020 Q3. They've never met a material projection yet. It seems Adam and Andrew are in this predicament because they never listened to their CFO before. It is doubtful that these tigers will be able to change their stripes. The only scenario in which I see a positive outlook for MedMen is if its Board changes the tigers and enters Cannabis 3.0 with a whole new executive team. You know, clean house.

In short, MedMen's problems seem to be rooted in the hubris of its founders who, by all accounts, lack any relevant experience in running large enterprises. (I wonder if they ever had to make payroll in their previous lives.) Instead of *butting heads* with their first few CFOs, including being sued by at least one of them (in addition to being sued by shareholders), they should have *listened* to their CFOs. It is apparent to me that Medmen's shareholders, customers and employees will be best served if MedMen's young leaders are replaced with experienced professionals.

COMPANY J: THE PETER PRINCIPLE

As Cannabis 2.0 fever was heating up in the Summer of 2018, many cannabis industry entrepreneurs pictured themselves as a CEO in the corner office of a publicly-held company, not having the vaguest idea of the scrutiny, rigor, discipline, and transparency in which publicly-held companies operate. Let's just say that most of these entrepreneurs do things as privately-held companies that you can't do as a publicly-held company.

They aren't used to operating in a glass house where their integrity is perpetually on display for all to see. They aren't used to the responsibility of being a fiduciary for their shareholders and other stakeholders and putting their interests before their own in all they do. They aren't used to opening their financial kimonos to investors or having shareholders in their underwear. That's the way it is in most small businesses. There is a small circle of folks that need to know about the financials: only the owner, his or her accountant, and Uncle Sam. And Uncle Sam should know as little as possible.

Cannabis 2.0 companies would be better served if its executives adopted the core values of the Air Force:

- Integrity first
- Service before self
- Excellence in all you do

Cannabis 2.0 companies sorely lack these core values of the Air Force. The investors and experienced CFO of Company J, which was gearing up for an RTO, continually coached the company's founders on things that will need to change before the company could become public. Things like being fully transparent, disclosing all related-party transactions, making sure that the actual *substance*, as well as the *appearance*, of all transactions are squeaky clean, and in general, over-communicating with auditors and legal advisors instead of hiding things from them. Regular communication with shareholders will also force discipline and transparency into cannabis company C-suites.

Company J's founders continued to hide various questionable actions and deals from their auditors and proceeded to enter into multiple questionable, often undocumented deals. The company rarely conducted due diligence despite repeated warnings from their internal and third-party legal counsels. Forced to sell to a competitor at a fraction of the value they could have garnered had they been able to change their stripes, Company J was never able to achieve the level of transparency and integrity needed to operate as a publicly-held company. The "tone at the top" was unethical. They didn't have the chops to run a public company. They would have ended up in prison.

The management team of this company, while they fancy themselves as successful business people, became the *consolidatees*, and not the *consolidators*. And in a consolidating industry, if you are a consolidatee and not the consolidator, you are shortchanging your shareholders by untold hundreds of millions in shareholder value. Just as in other well-known consolidating industries like garbage, equipment rental, ambulance service, logistics, satellite and cable-TV, and many others, these budding cannabis entrepreneurs will succumb to the Peter Principle: people will rise to the level of their own incompetence. The Peter Principle is on full display in Cannabis 2.0 companies. Make no mistake, they may achieve a big payday for themselves and be set for life, but they've peaked.

Think about it. What does a dry-cleaner operator, for example, know about managing complex entities? These inexperienced, "right-place, right-time" entrepreneurs are just as lucky as Hunter Biden who reportedly rode his father's coattails in several international blockbuster deals including a) being paid over $50,000 per month to sit on the Board of Burisma Holdings, a Ukrainian energy company, despite reportedly knowing next to nothing about the international energy industry, b) negotiating a $1.5 billion investment deal with the State Bank of China, and c) reportedly serving as legal counsel for a Romanian real-estate tycoon accused of orchestrating a corrupt land deal.

The only other character I know of with this breadth of visibility on the world-stage is *Forrest Gump*. He lived a storied life. Among other things, Forrest played football at the University of Alabama, met JFK, received the Medal of Honor from LBJ, and was selected to join the U.S. Army ping-pong team to play against his China counterparts.[25] Right place at the right time for sure.

Do these early-stage Cannabis 2.0 entrepreneurs know how to value acquisitions? Do they realize the infrastructure that is needed to scale a business? Do they understand what GAAP accounting is? Do they have dedicated Mergers and Acquisition (M&A) personnel experienced in the identification, valuation, negotiation, and integration of deals? Or do they ballpark deals and then punt the mess over to other folks in their companies who already have full-time jobs and never integrated acquisitions before? Do they know how to access capital and vet reputable investment bankers and financiers? Can they build the teams in the various business functions necessary to survive, let alone thrive and take advantage of the opportunities in this explosive cannabis industry? Do they know that they must shift from self-promotion with outlandish, unattainable financial projections to putting forth credible projections and gaining the trust of the investment community, which will most certainly hold them accountable? Do they know the importance of internal controls, and do they have a sufficient internal control framework in their own companies to prevent them from putting their companies in undesirous and risky situations in which they should never find themselves?

Are they strategic or opportunistic? If they operate opportunistically, expect chaos, disorganization, and seat-of-the-pants decision making without any analysis. They are guessing. In quickly growing, land grab types of industries (and Cannabis 2.0 falls in this category), even the most organized professionals are hard-pressed to implement strategic plans and stay the course.

Several public companies, like Canopy Growth and MedMen, and even some private companies have compensation expenses that are larger than their revenues! Only in Cannabis 2.0 and Hooterville can a get-rich-quick scheme like this exist. It's a quick hitter for the execs, a drive-by shooting for the shareholders, but the shareholders may not even be aware of the fleecing to which they are being subjected. This is not sustainable. This is not shareholder value-maximizing. This is not okay.

Yet still, these entrepreneurs beg for the markets to take them seriously and beg for legitimacy; however, through both their actions and inactions (i.e., errors of both commission and omission), they prove that they have not earned the legitimacy they seek.

Those entrepreneurs without a strategic north star (and frequently with a defective moral compass) will flail and flounder among the industry's flotsam and jetsam in shark-infested waters. Another Forrest Gump*ism* is appropriate: "Stupid is as stupid does."[26]

Company K: License applications — Gamesmanship or Fraud?

To be successful in winning licenses, you need to have the right combination of capital, operating experience, application submission expertise, and an experienced management team. But if you don't have these things, another method that is popular in the cannabis industry is just to *lie* on a license application. Cannabis license application submissions vary from accurate to misleading to outright fraudulent. The whole process is a game, and so, an experienced applications writer (usually an attorney) will help a company navigate through, and even game, the application process, turning a borderline application into a winner. Each category of the application (management team, financial strength, community outreach, social benevolence, etc.) receives a point score. The license winners are those entities that receive the highest overall points. Of course, there is a lot of gamesmanship and wordsmithing involved to be legally accurate, but many applications contain purposefully misleading or untruthful representations to garner a higher score from the various state's cannabis commission's reviewers.

Another common practice used by Cannabis 2.0 companies when completing state cannabis applications is to find resident strawmen in the states that the company is seeking a license.

Most states require nexus in the form of individuals having state residency when applying for licenses. Outside entities with no connection to the state need not apply. As such, the applying entity needs to find state residents to work with them in the application process.

Typically, the applying company and these strawmen with the requisite state residency form an LLC and enter into an agreement whereby, if they win the application, the strawmen will receive payment for their services for being a "placeholder." In exchange, the strawmen agree to transfer their legal interest in the LLC to the company as soon as permitted by the state's regulations. Some of these post-win transfer arrangements are documented, others are not. I've seen companies which have used resident strawmen end up winning licenses and, then, these strawmen, in the absence of a written agreement with the company, move the goalposts, effectively extorting millions of dollars more than was originally "agreed to" before selling their interest in the LLC back to the company.

Sometimes unscrupulous executives use shareholder funds to apply for licenses in their own name and then try to hide such use of shareholder funds and personal enrichment from auditors and other shareholders. To me, it sounds like what happened at Enron. In one company, a C-level executive told her CFO, "hide this from the auditors," in referring to a paper trail that implicated the CEO in using company funds to apply for a license in her name personally (and not in the company's name). That doesn't sound above board to me, and it shouldn't to you either.

Maybe she'll get caught, perhaps not, but do you want your management team putting the company (and your investment as a shareholder) at risk like this? This is an excellent example of something that some ethically-challenged entrepreneurs might attempt in privately-held companies that they can't afford to do in a company with many shareholders counting on them to act as a fiduciary on their behalf.

Company K completed various state cannabis applications and to garner the highest score in the applications' financial strength sections, its founder personally attested he *had unencumbered access to $80 million of liquid cash.* Not cash in short-term investments, not cash that didn't belong to him or is an asset of another company, but liquid cash sitting in a money-market, certificate of deposit or bank account. I'm not quite sure if this is a badge of honor or an indication of fiscal stupidity. (i.e., Who keeps such large sums of money in a bank account earning next to nothing? Not sure I'd be bragging about this.)

In any event, the founder probably thought that since his *company* recently raised $80 million (which was properly shown as cash on the balance sheet of the holding company), that this money was *his*, personally. Additionally, unless there was actually $160 million floating around, the funds can only be shown in one place — either on the balance sheet of the company or as an asset of the owner, but not both. Since the *company* raised the $80 million, of course it properly belongs on its books. As such, the founder is incorrect when he asserted on the state license applications that he has "unencumbered access to $80 million in liquid cash."

This was inexperienced, naïve chest-pounding by an owner who didn't understand the separation of personal affairs from business affairs and the serious consequences of making such a brazen misrepresentation on a state cannabis application license. I guess he figured he wouldn't get caught or that he had a good excuse if or when he was. This inexperienced owner freely co-mingled personal and business expenses in his privately-held endeavors in his previous life to suit his particular needs at the time, so why not do it here? Instead of giving the applicant high scores for financial strength, a smart regulator should have flagged this absurd claim as being suspicious or deceitful and deduct points or disqualify the application altogether.

Like a college admissions scandal that displaces deserving students from being admitted, companies which cheat on cannabis license applications and are awarded a license displace other worthy companies from being awarded a license — like those who will lose hundreds of thousands of dollars spent on application costs by playing by the rules. Pure greed. Money hungry. How do these people sleep at night? They give the industry a black-eye. Unfortunately, the industry is full of them.

COMPANY L: BAIT AND SWITCH — A BOGUS STOCK OPTION PLAN

Another "buyer beware" area of corporate governance in Cannabis 2.0 is in the field of employment agreements and equity compensation plans. These issues are complex enough when professionals deal with professionals, but even more so when professionals negotiate with inexperienced, greedy, and inept founders. After all, not too many small business entrepreneurs turned cannabis company owners have any experience in attracting professionals into their coffee shop business by offering stock options.

Let's examine the case of Company L, an aspiring MSO with operations in several states with the plan to do an RTO. As such, it had to attract professionals from across several functions: sales, accounting, operations, marketing, and more. If you have been fortunate enough to have had stock options, restricted stock, phantom stock, profits interest plans, or similar plans, you know how complicated these can be. You also know how to play the game: take a less-than-market salary and plan on busting your ass for a few years in exchange for the opportunity to participate in any number of stock incentive plans common to start-ups. If properly structured, the employee will share in the increase of the shareholder wealth he or she helped create. For sure, employees in start-ups are taking on significant risks and there is no guarantee the company will survive or that the employees will receive their just rewards. (**Author's note:** While I've been fortunate to have enjoyed a half-dozen or so equity events, I've also come up with an equal number of goose eggs along the way.)

Further, venture and private equity investors worth their salt will *insist* that these companies incent their key employees by having them aligned with the shareholders. And what a better way to do this than to have a form of equity compensation plan in place. I won't bore you with all the academic studies that conclude shareholder return is enhanced when key management receive incentives through equity participation. Companies know that when everyone is rowing in the same direction and incented with some meaningful wealth-creating opportunities that they will bust their asses. Who benefits? The shareholders, and when shareholders benefit, and if these plans are structured correctly, the employees are also sure to win. Capitalism is a great thing: reward excellent performance leading to shareholder value creation. It makes you work hard, putting pride in your work instead of mailing it in. Capitalism makes the world go around.

Typically, the percentage of outstanding shares that are set aside for management equity incentive plans (called an "overhang") is in the 15 - 20% range, depending on industry and market conditions. Some customary rules of thumb exist. For instance, a CFO is typically granted shares equating to 2% of the company's outstanding shares in the early stages. A COO might get 3-5%. Another rule of thumb is that the share price at various stages of a company's growth should continue to rise. While this isn't always the case, typically, a company's earliest employees' stock options are more valuable than those who come later to the party.

I've been part of several companies that granted stock options to *all* employees. Sometimes even administrative assistants made millions because they were among the company's first employees with stock options issued for pennies per share. As such, when the company IPO'd at, say, $22 a share, they were instant millionaires. They made more than some other employees who filled more senior positions but came later. These folks deserve every penny they earned for taking the risk (and in almost all cases, at less than a market salary) early in a company's life when its future prospects are not guaranteed. Better than winning the lottery, for sure.

Another feature of employee stock equity plans is that the equity "vests" to the employee over, typically, two to four years. This vesting cements the employee-employer relationship, incenting good employees to continue to work hard so they can continue to vest more equity. Vesting typically begins when the employee starts. That's the attractiveness of early-stage companies:

get in early and begin to vest in stock options which should become more valuable through the employee's efforts and long hours in helping build value for the shareholders. Another benefit of vesting from the company's perspective is that it makes it hard for good employees to move to a competitor while his or her equity is still being vested. (After all, why would someone leave if they have yet to accumulate significant wealth through the vesting of additional shares? And, why would the company want the employee to leave if he is moving the needle and creating value?)

It is customary that vesting schedules for early-stage companies provide for an accelerated 100% vesting of all unvested shares in the event a sale of the company or a change of control occurs. The reason is because it provides a safety net and fair compensation to the employee if selling the company is the path which maximizes shareholder value. (i.e., If vesting did not automatically accelerate to 100% when a potential suitor came forth with a value-maximizing acquisition offer, the company's management might be reluctant to entertain a sale of the company for fear of putting themselves out of a job.) But do the mom-and-pops running these cannabis companies and their lawyers realize this?

Back to Company L. The founder of Company L was not familiar with equity plans and has never worked in a company with equity plans. Nor had she ever participated in equity compensation plans. Additionally, she never realized that there is a quid-pro-quo when asking professionals to join your company at 50% of the market salary. It's a package deal: reduced salary in exchange for participation in a stock compensation plan. You can't ask employees to take a reduced salary and not deliver on the stock compensation plan. To do so is unethical. Greedy.

Company L did not have an equity plan in place, but its founder represented to eligible potential employees that the company is "working with its attorneys in putting the final touches on its equity plan." So, in the interim, the employment agreements of Company L stated that the employee would "be able to participate in the equity plans as developed and determined by the Board of Directors." This assurance seemed good enough for most potential employees, and so they signed up with Company L while they understood the company continued to work in good faith in finalizing the equity compensation plan. (It is likely that Company L's attorneys carefully crafted the actual language used in the representations made to prospective employees regarding the equity compensation plan to allow her an "out" should she not choose to operate in good faith or if she has a defective *ethics* gene.)

By dangling the promise of being able to participate in a stock option plan, she was able to attract much needed experienced professionals who added credibility and legitimacy to her team. As each week passed, the company became more valuable due to the efforts of these employees who were working at 50% market salaries believing the promises of stock options by the founder. Naturally, from time-to-time, the employees inquired as to the status and terms of the equity plan. The founder told employees that the company had hired a compensation consulting firm to implement the promised stock option plan.

More days, weeks, and months passed with the company increasing in value, but still no plan. A lot of wealth was being created for the existing shareholders by underpaid executives promised shares in the value they created, but they had nothing to show for it. No vesting was taking place.

After about six months, a public company approached Company L with a proposal to buy it. The offer was in the several hundred-million-dollar range. While the value of the company increased over 10x, the employees who were promised equity had none. They were given the shaft: over six months of seventy-plus hour work weeks at 50% of market salaries without the ability to share in the increased value of the company that they were largely responsible for creating. This was not what they (or their families) signed up for. The founder avoided the employees' inquiries as to how, when, or if they would receive compensation for driving shareholder value into the stratosphere. Having broken her promise to implement a stock option plan for individual key employees, she had painted herself into a corner and became reclusive. This is what happens when one doesn't keep promises, is greedy, and lacks integrity. Just lie and then hide.

The founder kept stringing employees along by now saying that the employees would participate in the existing equity plan of the acquiring company. She kept telling employees, "I'll take care of you," but without some concrete plan, her promises rang hollow.

News of the company's sale and that the founder would not honor her equity plan promises to many employees spread quickly. The employees who were promised equity couldn't take a joke anymore. There was outright panic and mutiny in the workforce. Even those never promised equity saw the founder's real colors, and they realized they were working for someone who was only in it for herself.

Company L's inexpert founder never intended to implement the employee stock equity plan she had represented. A bait-and-switch. In the end, she was just greedy. Money-hungry. She saw an equity incentive plan, not as a powerful incentive earned by loyal employees to generate the super-human performance to create significant shareholder value creation, but instead, as dilutive to the value of her own personal stake. Pigs get fat, and hogs get slaughtered. Yes, I am *equity shaming* her.

Chuck, an employee who was promised participation in an equity plan and who spent a lot of time on the road, called into the switchboard from the road and said, "Put the Jew on the phone!" in reference to the founder's religious background. Chuck told the founder, "You better not screw me on this sale." Trying to buy herself time until she had a solution, she laughed it off, telling Chuck, "Don't worry, I'll take care of you."

Another employee, a C-level executive, had enough of her stall tactics. Still getting the runaround, he pressed her to explain exactly how the stock plan would work in light of the company's pending sale. Still getting vague promises with no path to the equity promised to him, he faced a choice: continue to work for peanuts, making others rich, or cut his losses, quit, and find another company in the cannabis industry that "gets it" and understands the value of C-level experience in growing a company. And that is precisely what he did. Like LeBron James, he took his talents elsewhere. He quit, got another C-level job in the industry within a week, and one with a 2% equity stake, which began vesting immediately. For that C-level executive, working at Company L for an owner lacking a moral compass and integrity turned out to be a tremendous waste of time.

Because Company L's CEO didn't value him and "lock him up" with an equity plan, he felt no loyalty whatsoever towards her and her empty equity promises. His leaving came at an inopportune time as the company was in the midst of a sale. Besides the work they needed to do, his resignation sent a tremendously negative signal to the acquiring company, and they had to scramble to fill the void.

As other employees began to realize that there would be no stock option plan before the sale of the company, many told her, "fuck you" and jumped ship. Why continue busting your ass for this greedy *bastardette* for a goose egg? Had employees known up front that the promised stock option plan was just a charade, they wouldn't have signed up with Company L in the first place.

Clearly, the CEO was wet behind the ears when it came to promising stock options to individual key employees. The employees who were promised equity via a stock plan lent their names, experience, and biographies to the company's websites and pitch decks. Their experience added legitimacy and credibility to the company and the founder's relatively weak expertise. They were a primary reason why investors invested in the company in the first place. These experienced executives de-risk the investment calculus because they increase the company's probability it will be able to execute its plan. These "been there, done that executives" are a huge reason, if not *the* main reason, why Company L attracted investors and why its valuation grew wildly.

Company L benefitted from their experience and from saving 50% on the cash cost of these salaries. A lot of people were screwed on this deal, except for Company L's CEO and shareholders, who were able to avoid a mere 10% dilution event from the implementation of the promised stock option plan. Call it a switcheroo, bait and switch, or whatever — this is a lawsuit waiting to happen, and yet one more reason why D&O insurance is prohibitively expensive for cannabis companies.

This is more than an innocent mistake by Company L's founder. This is bush league — pure greed. Company L used people. It hired much-needed professionals and promised these professionals something that it had no intention of fulfilling. I guess she didn't care about her integrity or reputation when she took her share of the hundreds of millions of proceeds from the sale of the company to the bank.

Do you think the folks at Google who have toiled for years did so in the hopes that one day they would finally get equity only when Google goes public in an IPO? No. They were granted options at the price of the stock when they were first employed: substantially lower than the price when the company goes public. Stock Compensation 101. This is how the game is played in the real world. Unfortunately, some Cannabis 2.0 entrepreneurs do not understand this. Worse yet, they don't care to.

Being that she would walk away with somewhere in the neighborhood of a hundred million, you would think that Company L's founder could have kept her promise and given her team, in the words of groundskeeper Carl Spackler in *Caddyshack,* "you know, a little something for the effort."[27]

Contrast this greed with the generosity of an individual I once worked for who sold a privately-held logistics company for over $300 million. He carved out $30 million to reward his key employees. Quite an enormous thank you indeed. I'm sure he sleeps well at night knowing he treated others fairly.

COMPANY M: A MEETING TO MURDER BRUCE

One would think that with millions of dollars to be made in Cannabis 2.0 that everyone would stay in their own lanes, focus, and soldier on; after all, there are millions to be made, correct? Like the California gold rush: "There's gold in them thar hills."

And, like the California gold rush, greed is rampant. During the Gold Rush, people were pick-axed and shot to death to protect one's claim that they staked. Same in the Dot.com era (sans pick-axe) and now the same in the cannabis industry. And this brings me to my favorite story of how far folks go in Cannabis 2.0 to protect what they believe is "rightfully theirs."

Many Cannabis 2.0 companies are built by spirited entrepreneurs who cobbled together a little piece of this and a little bit of that. Synergies abound when the holder of a grow/cultivation license, for example, joins forces with a holder of several dispensary licenses. Similarly, geographic expansion into new states is also facilitated when cannabis entrepreneurs partner up. These partnerships and joint ventures often bring together people who, other than being in the burgeoning cannabis industry, may not have a lot in common. They may be of different nationalities or different cultures. One may be strategic, the other opportunistic; one divorced, the other a family man; one a cokehead and a drunk, the other strait-laced. The point is that the cannabis industry is a blender, and the entrepreneurs are the ingredients that may or may not blend well together.

You've no doubt heard the adage "never go into business with friends or family." Well, if true, then all that is left is to go into business with strangers, unknown quantities. Despite agreements, contracts, and other lawyerly documents, the truth is that you don't know what you don't know about somebody until it's too late. Then, you wish you knew earlier. Such is the case in the cannabis industry. Take Company M, for instance.

Its founders could be considered successful if success means obtaining grow/cultivation licenses in a few different states. In the course of selling its weed, Company M had to sell through a network of dispensaries. As such, partnerships were destined to be formed. And, so began a relationship from hell.

Steve and Bruce joined forces in Nevada. The way Bruce tells it, Steve was an outcast from his family's business — a regional industrial services company. The way Steve tells it is that Bruce was out to screw everyone in his way. As with most things, the truth usually lies somewhere in the middle.

The two formed holding companies to hold the licenses for their cultivation centers and dispensaries. In no time, Steve went out to run the company's Arizona operations, and before long, the War of the Roses began. $100,000 of sexual harassment lawsuit settlements later, Bruce took over control and told Steve to "stand down" and never go to Arizona again. Of course, there are two sides to every story, and it was soon apparent that Steve was not a fan of Bruce's either. Bruce continued to build the master plan to take Company M public, and that would require Steve's consent to contribute his share of the companies he owned with Bruce to a newly formed parent holding company. At first, Steve did not want to roll-up his ownership rights. Steve thought that the valuation formula which Bruce used in valuing the companies he was rolling-up led to a low-ball valuation and so he went into radio silence with respect to rolling-up his companies. Bruce knew that without Steve's consent to roll-up his companies like the other companies had already done, Steve could queer the deal for everyone. A stalemate took place. Steve knew that he had leverage, and Bruce would need to cut a sweeter deal with him. Steve was in no hurry while Bruce was getting more desperate with each passing day because he had a timeline to meet. Various, but unsuccessful, attempts to agree to terms took place with the lawyers from both sides playing *fuck you* with each other.

After a few months without any forward progress, Steve invited Bruce to his office for a hastily arranged, impromptu meeting to discuss the stalemate. Bruce, really needing Steve to agree to the deal, grabbed his right-hand man, Darren, at the last minute to accompany him to the meeting at Steve's office.

The meeting got heated, and punches were thrown. The meeting ended abruptly when Steve's associate pulled out a gun. *Really? A gun?* Was this a pre-planned meeting to kill Bruce? Bruce and Darren ran out of the office, jumped into their car, no doubt with their hearts racing, and escaped with their lives.

They weren't sure if Steve was drunk, deranged, or even if he was of sound mind and body. Of course, it could be that Bruce poked the bear one too many times or was just a bully himself, and it was time for some payback. In any event, no one was wounded or dead, and it didn't make the evening news (or an episode of *Dateline*). Darren believed that if he hadn't attended the meeting that he was pretty sure that Steve would have killed Bruce. In the end, Bruce now had leverage on Steve. Bruce filed a police report, and Steve eventually came to his senses and agreed to contribute his shares to the roll-up.

Let's put the FUN back into dysFUNctional!

(**Author's note:** I'm usually not one to poke fun at attempted homicides, but I will anyway. This story highlights the need for background checks and the mandated waiting period when buying a gun. It reminds me of an episode of *The Simpsons* in which Bart visits a local gun shop to purchase a firearm. Bart wanted to buy a gun and take it home with him the same day. The gun shop owner explained to Bart, "The law requires a five-day waiting period. We've got to run a background check." A frustrated Bart replies, "Five days? *But I'm mad now!*"[28])

Company N: The rules don't apply to us!

Thank goodness that the Illinois' Compassionate Use Blah Blah Act requires that *a bonafide physician-patient relationship* exists before a doctor approves the patient for a state-issued medical marijuana card. (There wouldn't be doctors trying to game the system, now would there? Wink-wink.) Here's the relevant excerpt from the Act:

> *"Bonafide physician-patient relationship" means a relationship established at a hospital, physician's office, or other health care facility in which the physician has an ongoing responsibility for the assessment, care, and treatment of a patient's debilitating medical condition or a symptom of the patient's debilitating medical condition.*[29]

The good state of Illinois doesn't want sham doctors who can write a script without a valid medical need. The state doesn't want a repeat of the opioid mill doctors who found ways to prescribe thousands of pills to individuals causing an untold social catastrophe. It doesn't want a doctor to have the ability to meet someone in a bar and authorize that person for a medical marijuana card. No. The state requires a legitimate physician-patient relationship to exist. It says so right there in the statute in black and white. Of course, sham doctors issuing medical marijuana cards without a legitimate medical necessity would never happen in the world of medical marijuana, would it? As it turns out, it would.

Company N is located in a medical marijuana state with the same "bonafide physician-patient relationship" language as Illinois'. Its CEO brought in a doctor to its corporate offices for the purpose of helping its employees obtain medical marijuana cards. So right from the start, this arrangement violates the state's laws because the doctor will be performing the medical exams outside of the physician's office. As such, the required "bonafide physician-patient" relationship per this particular state's statute is circumvented. It sure seems that the CEO's purpose in inviting the doctor to Company N's corporate office is so its employees can get medical marijuana cards to purchase marijuana — not for any legitimate medical use, but — *just because.* This is what this state's laws are trying to prevent.

But here we have a CEO who passed a background check with the state and is licensed by the state to own cultivation centers and dispensaries who knowingly conspired with a quack doctor to circumvent the state's medical marijuana statues. Supposedly the state would expect the CEO to act with integrity as an essential cog in its medical marijuana ecosystem. Apparently, this CEO thinks otherwise. The CEO is an enabler.

From conversations with cannabis company insiders in medical-only states, they estimate that at least two-thirds of their employees carry state medical issued cards, whereas the general penetration rate of state-issued medical marijuana cards to the state's total populace is about 1%. This delta is statistically significant: the disproportionate amount of dispensary employees who apparently need medical marijuana versus the general populace can't be statistically explained. There must be other reasons that cause this phenomenon — like the actions of CEOs like Company N's who conspired with irreputable doctors to circumvent state statutes and make it easy for their employees to obtain medical marijuana cards, regardless of medical necessity.

Why did he do this? Why would Company N's CEO risk his company's valuable license only to endear himself to his employees by facilitating their ability to get medical marijuana cards? (Kinda like a parent being a cool friend to his or her kids instead of being a parent, don't cha think?)

Even more surprising is that Company N does not have private offices in which to conduct the appropriate physician-patient consultations: all the offices have glass windows and doors. No place to perform an examination. Just a place to talk. Is that all that is required for a (quack) doctor to issue a medical marijuana card? Any HIPAA violations here?

Are the employees, the doctors, or both "manufacturing" illnesses which qualify "patients" for medical marijuana cards? Is the doctor being paid by Company N or by the employees (that is, the "patients")? Is the doctor legit, or instead, is he under pressure from the CEO to manufacture diseases to qualify as many employees as possible for medical cards? Does this "arranged marriage" between employee and the company-endorsed doctor qualify as "*a bonafide physician-patient relationship*" as per the letter and spirit of the state statute?

I find it interesting that this particular state's statute does not list "cannabis company corporate offices" in the definition of approved locations where a *bonafide physician-patient relationship* can be established. Just saying. Does the doctor know this? Does the CEO know this? Do the CEO's shareholders know what their CEO is doing?

What would the state regulators whose jobs are to enforce their state's medical marijuana Act do if they investigated this? Would they sanction the company? Shut it down? Throw the CEO in the clink? Look the other way? This is yet another example of a green CEO jeopardizing his livelihood in the industry and putting his company and shareholders at risk. He acts entitled as if the rules don't apply to him. Is this the level of maturity and leadership in which you want to invest? A reckless cowboy?

I think it's a fair observation that there isn't a lot of "doctoring" going on in these consultation meetings. It's a joke. The consultations last as little as ten minutes. It is an overreach to call many of these "doctors," doctors. They are quacks. Just as the opioid pill mill doctors exploit the FDA, these doctors' entire business model is to game the medical marijuana system. They have a cozy relationship with the dispensaries that, in turn, steer patients their way. They are to dispensaries what puppy mills are to pet stores. They are quack doctors and frauds.

It's an end-result in search of a disease. The end-result being: "let's qualify this person for legalized cannabis." The process is that the doctor must, in his professional opinion, of course, choose from a few dozen ailments. For instance, one employee at Company N, Danny, played sports in high school. During the consultation, the doctor determined that Danny needs marijuana to treat the effects of concussions he may have suffered from his involvement in sports a dozen years ago. Danny's sport in high school? He ran track.

I doubt that Danny ever received a concussion while running track. Methinks that Danny doesn't have a qualifying medical condition but that he just wants to buy some weed so he and his friends can smoke a bowl on the back porch. Lanna, another Company N employee, got her medical marijuana card after being diagnosed by the good doctor with PTSD. You ask: "PTSD? I wonder what war she was in?" In the case of Lanna, she wasn't in a war at all. Then you ask, "What was the source of her PTSD?" Through either great psychic abilities or sleuthing that would make Columbo proud, the quack doctor traced Lanna's PTSD back to the divorce of her parents some twenty years ago! Why, of course! Apparently, this is nothing a couple of bongs can't cure. What is even more amazing than this inciteful diagnosis is that Lanna was able to survive the past twenty years at all without medical marijuana to ease her pain. She must have blocked this trauma from her conscious mind — how she must have suffered.

But I jest. Indeed, legitimate, competent doctors and patients who require the benefits for which medical marijuana programs have been put in place do exist. My examples demonstrate how dubious actors game the system. While the legislators like to believe that 100% of their state's issued medical marijuana cards are legitimate, it may pain them if they were to find out that doctors are approving *patients* to obtain medical marijuana cards so that folks can continue to legally carry-on their college or high school habits.

It's kind of like getting an annulment in the Catholic Church. It seems that an annulment in the Catholic Church starts with the premise that there must have been a *defect* in the marriage to cause a divorce. Maybe one of the recipients of the Blessed Sacrament of Marriage was an alcoholic? A wife-beater? Or, could it be that, simply, *things just didn't work out.* The priest in the annulment process begins with the premise: "We need to annul this marriage." He then goes on to interview and develop a fact pattern that fits the narrative and the result sought. Like an impeachment in search of a crime: find supporting evidence to fit the desired narrative.

COMPANY O: THE BIG SWINGING DICK

There is a difference between investors who invest in a company to operate it in the long term vs. those who invest for a quick hitter: to flip it like the many *Flip This House* shows on cable TV. There are a few investors, in particular, whose only goal was to get a quick hit — to invest and sell. Similar to investors who flipped houses circa 2006 until they could flip no more.

Company O had a few investors who were opportunistic, greedy, naïve, desperate, or all the above. These investors, as the story goes, recently came off a cannabis company home run with a quick hitter in 2017. They turned a $10 million investment in the nascent cannabis industry into hundreds of millions in less than a year. Right place, right time. Better to be lucky than good. With this "fuck you money," they went out and bought the obligatory corporate jet so they can parlay another small investment into an even bigger home run — a grand slam this time.

By mid-2018, the cannabis industry was red hot for the next RTO. The company they had been courting, however, was in no shape to be taken public on the Canadian Stock Exchange in an RTO. The problem was, like many other Cannabis 2.0 companies, Company O was run like a frat house, and the books and records were in no shape to be audited. Some investors are called whales; others are commonly known as a BSD — a Big Swinging Dick (emphasis on *Dick*). In 2018 Q2, one BSD implored Company O to hire a CFO to prepare the company to go public. They hired the CFO, and in turn, she immediately hired rooms full of accountants and auditors to get the books in shape. The fact that Company O's founders had no experience in preparing a company for a public offering meant that it was a work-in-progress and would take nine to twelve months of balls-to-the-wall work to get this company ready.

After the BSD from Colorado ponied up a $5 million investment, he held a conference call with Company O's management team to mark his territory in terms of expectations going forward. They held the conference call on July 17. Before the call, the young founders asked their CFO for her best guesstimate as to when the audit would be complete. The audit was a gating critical path item towards going public. Having been around the block a few times and this not being her first rodeo, the CFO estimated "between Thanksgiving and Christmas," which, incidentally, is about the worst time possible to take a company public with all the holidays getting in the way. Internally, she knew this is not what the owners would want to hear, and that this timeline was very aggressive with less than a 50% chance of being met.

On the call, the BSD queried the CFO for her best guess as to a date when the audit would be completed. The CFO responded, "December 1." (Notice she was not careful to commit to which year!) They heard a full rebuttal on the conference call from the BSD: "***Wrong!*** The date for completion will be August 31. We need to hit this red-hot market."

The CFO started to explain (and later got chastised for it by the founders) that "in a perfect world, we might be able to meet that date if this was the second time auditing the company" (which wasn't the case); "and if we know that all legal documents supporting dozens of transactions exist" (which there could be no assurance with so many legal entities and about a hundred shareholders); "and if we know that we can find all supporting documents, receipts, tax returns, invoices, bank statements, and payrolls" (which was doubtful);

"and if the company is properly staffed to support an audit" (which it wasn't); "and if the company's outside accountants could produce consolidated statements" (which they already demonstrated they hadn't the foggiest notion of how to consolidate financial statements); "and if the company had nothing else to do while the audit was occurring" (which wasn't the case as the founders were busy acquiring companies); "and . . . " Shall I continue? Get the picture? The fact is that the unaudited financial statements that had been previously prepared and served as the basis for the BSD's investment weren't worth the paper they were written on! The CFO thought, "We'll be lucky to complete the audit by Christmas!"

Despite these facts, the BSD told the team assembled on the conference call that "the audit deadline *will* be met." Because they didn't know what they don't know, the founders had no idea what was feasible or not, so they expected the audit to be completed by August 31, only forty-five days from the call, just as the BSD dictated. Nothing but wishful thinking.

The owners thought, "How hard could an audit be? It's just paperwork. We'll hire more auditors, and they can work at night to compress calendar time to complete the audit." Was the BSD trying to intimidate or motivate the team with his "land a man on the moon by the end of the decade" edict? Perhaps he floated August 31 as a trial balloon, keeping his "whisper number" date of September 30 in his back pocket? (Not that this date was achievable either.) Maybe he was clueless? In any event, the BSD's intimidation or ignorance did nothing to promote morale and open lines of communication. It only showed his naïveté concerning taking companies public.

Fast forward: Company O's audit was not signed off on by the auditors until April 2019 — some *nine* months later. *Missed it by that much.*

COMPANY P: LAWSUITS-A-PLENTY

I don't know of any Cannabis 2.0 companies that aren't facing material lawsuits: whether from investors, employees, partners, regulators, sore losers from the application process — whomever. These lawsuits are classic, textbook quality Venn diagram depictions of greed intersecting with inexperienced management and owners. A perfect storm.

In the second half of 2018, Company P won about eight dispensary licenses in a limited license state.

> Some states, including Nevada, Illinois, and others, are known as limited license states, meaning that they grant only a certain number of licenses to operate in the state. Owning one of these licenses in limited license states is almost certainly a green light to mint money. Contrast this to cannabis licensure in Colorado, for example, where just about anyone who wants to open a dispensary can open one. Competition among Colorado's over 900 dispensaries is fierce, as evidenced by relatively low prices and margins. Because of this, you won't find many MSOs interested in owning assets in Colorado. The reason? Colorado has very few barriers to entry compared with substantial barriers to entry in limited license states, making licenses in limited license states countlessly more valuable.

Within about ten nanoseconds after the announcement of the winners, several applicants who did not win a license filed lawsuits with the state claiming the state did not fairly score the applications in determining the winners. This isn't the only state where there are sore losers. New Jersey, Nevada, and nearly every other state that awards cannabis licenses have also come under scrutiny and challenges after the announcement of state cannabis license application winners.

The whole system is smoke and mirrors: applicants hire high-priced legal firms who know how to play the game and where to bend the rules, and if necessary, where to outright lie to maximize points on the application. Call me old-fashioned, but I've always thought that when completing state or federal forms that all answers should be factual and legally accurate. Of course, wordsmithing can position the applicant in the best light, and there are ways to do this while being legally accurate. Think of Clinton in his deposition: "It depends on what the meaning of the word 'is' is."[30]

The problem is that, once the puffery starts, it doesn't stop. *What's the harm in a little exaggerating? After all, everyone does it.*

In addition to lawsuits associated with license applications, lawsuits have been filed or threatened to be filed against Company P by vendors for non-payment, by employees for broken promises, and by shareholders for various reasons. Company P did not have D&O insurance.

Company P is not alone in getting sued. In addition to many product liability, employee, and shareholder lawsuits, predictably law firms with an eye on class action lawsuits are initiating securities fraud investigations. As such, these law firms are looking to speak with potential plaintiffs who have suffered financial losses. In November 2019, one such firm, Hagens Berman Sobol Shapiro, LLP, urged Aurora Cannabis Inc. investors who suffered losses to contact their firm. The Hagens Berman press release states, "The investigation centers on the accuracy of Aurora Cannabis' reported financial statements and purported progress in completing significant construction projects."[31] (Hmmm . . . inaccurate financial statements?) This is the tip of the iceberg. I bet that there is much below the surface too. These lawsuits have all the makings of taking down Titanics, and de-railing announced acquisitions. More to come.

COMPANY Q: SNAKE OIL

With everyone trying to cash in and make a quick buck in the cannabis industry, it's buyer beware! Cannabis and CBD product companies guide their customers concerning which products to buy for their particular ailments. Have a sore back? Try this one. Restless legs? Here's the one for you. Cancer, inflammation, irritable bowel? Here ya' go! Something for everyone. Like one of Mr. Haney's many elixirs on *Green Acres*, these cannabis and CBD companies are peddling cures for whatever ails you.

The problem is, it's mostly folklore and conjecture. It's anecdotal. Scant studies exist regarding the efficaciousness, bio-availability, and even the safety of many cannabis and CBD products. So, you're at the mercy of the marketing claims of these profit-driven companies and your own common sense. You're constantly finding yourself at the intersection of "Walk" and "Don't Walk."

I suffered from what I thought was a groin pull after a racquetball tournament. In January 2018, I convinced my college roommate, Kevin Wilkinson, to travel up to the Chicago area from his family and home near St. Louis to be my partner in the Illinois State Racquetball Association's (ISRA) 2018 men's doubles tournament. We would play in the C division in the 55-60 bracket. I envisioned how good that trophy would look next to my little league 3rd place trophy and my grade school band medals. Indeed, a great piece of hardware to add to my shrine of mediocrity.

My mind wandered to the prospects of winning: Would I remember to grab the trophy in my left hand, leaving my right hand available for shaking hands with the tournament director? Would I be asked to make a speech for winning the ISRA Men's Double 55-60 C division? Would Kevin and I split our allotted time on the speech? Would he go first? Would we be interviewed on *The Tonight Show* to talk about our great triumph? With this potential fame, I reminded myself that if we won, I would still try to be humble. I'd still put on my pants one leg at a time as the commoners do.

As it turned out, there were not enough participants in the tournament bracket for our age group and skill level, so the ISRA tournament director *collapsed* several brackets. We ended up playing with some 40-year-old young guns who were A-level players and who whipped us 15-5, 15-1. We ended up in fourth (i.e., last) place in the bracket. No trophies or medals for fourth place, just a crappy shirt. Hardly worth Kevin's time to drive up for the weekend (but at least he got a free tournament shirt to remember our epic fail). There would be no trophy, no speech, no appearance on *The Tonight Show*.

The other souvenir I received from the tournament was severe pain in my hip from diving on the floor. (As sore as I was, Kevin reported he had back pain after the tournament, claiming he had to carry me on his back during the entire competition!) The pain lasted days, then months, and soon a year.

I thought it was a muscle-related groin pull, so I had my doctor check it out. He ordered a hip x-ray and immediately diagnosed severe osteoarthritis. I thought that arthritis was something that only older people got. (*Hmmm . . . Never mind. I just answered my own question.*)

The doctor was surprised I could walk at all. I would need total hip replacement surgery soon. Additionally, while the hip pain was probably not related to any singular event like my loss in the ISRA Men's Double 55-60 C division, it certainly contributed to it. In the interim, I continued to endure moderate pain and limp a bit. My jogging, hockey and racquetball days were over. My golfing days were hanging on by a thread until I got a total hip replacement surgery.

Anyway, in the Spring of 2019, I mentioned my ailments to Larry, a twenty-something who was formulating CBD products for a West Coast-based cannabis and CBD company with whom I was working. What were Larry's qualifications? He was in a severe motorcycle accident and became addicted to opioids as part of his recovery. He was able to stop the downward spiral of opioids by stumbling upon various CBD products. Now, totally off of opioids, he began working at a CBD company under the direction of the Chief Science Officer who, unlike Larry, actually had a bunch of degrees and deep experience in pharma and food-grade products regulated by the FDA. By contrast, Larry didn't have any formal training in lab science or the like. He relied on a lot of personal research and a lot of folklore.

So, in discussing my ailments with Larry, I asked if any CBD products could help me. Kind of like a consultation with my doctor on my cholesterol issue, except Larry was not a doctor, was in his twenties, was wearing a tie-dye shirt, cut-offs, and flip flops instead of a white lab coat, and the consultation took place in a dark parking lot. Further, Larry had no formal experience in the science in which I was seeking his guidance. Shame on me. But that is how it is in the world of cannabis and CBD: more legend and mythology than facts.

Trying to be helpful, of course, Larry told me, "the reason you aren't getting better is that you continue to aggravate and inflame the muscles by continuing to exercise, walk, and do your normal things. You need to take this new anti-inflammatory CBD product we're developing to reduce the inflammation so that you give your body a chance to recover." I thought, "Of course. How could I have been so stupid? Of course, Larry was correct: I wasn't giving my body a chance to recover." Larry's advice sounded plausible to me. So, where do I sign up?

Larry gave me a brown vial with a handwritten label that said, "CBD anti-inflamatory" (misspelled and all). It reminded me of school lunches where my mom would write my name on the brown bag with a *Marks-A-Lot* marker. Nothing official about this vial of drugs that a twenty-something advised me to ingest during a conversation in a dark parking lot. When Larry gave me the sample, there was no consideration for dosing instructions as you'd see with any prescription regulated by the Food and Drug Administration. It was more or less as if he was giving me a recommendation or advice: "Try it this way, and if that doesn't work, then try a bit more before bed, and then when you wake up, etc." Because Larry only gave me a small sample, there wasn't a lot of CBD product there to begin with, so I only took a little each day.

After a week, despite following Larry's verbal instructions (as best as I could remember), I felt no improvement from the anti-inflammatory CBD compound. When I saw Larry, I told him, "The CBD you gave me did nothing for me." He asked how much I took and if I took it regularly. I advised that I skipped days here and there and only took it once a day on the days when I did take it.

Dr. Larry said that I didn't give my body enough time to feel the effects and told me to try it again, this time giving me more detailed instructions, albeit verbal, on how much and when to take it. He came back with another vial with more product in it. During the next week, I followed his instructions to the letter of what I remembered he told me to do. I took it twice a day as directed. Again, no effect. After I ran out of the product that he supplied, I tried a few Aleve to see if I could tell the difference between Aleve and the

CBD product from *Dr. Larry*. The Aleve noticeably relieved some of the pain from my fifty-eight-year-old shoddy hip.

The next week I saw the good *doctor* again. Larry asked, "How did it work out?" Again, I explained that even with following the new and improved verbal dosing instructions he provided, that the CBD had absolutely no effect toward relieving my pain. Maybe it works on others, but not on this washed-up Illinois State Racquetball Association Men's Double 55-60 Division C racquetball fourth-place finisher.

From then on, I took Aleve as instructed on the bottle by the good folks at Bayer. It worked like a charm. The pain was gone. My problem was solved until I got total hip replacement surgery. (**Author's note:** I had total hip replacement surgery in October 2019.)

Because there isn't a lot of scientific research on all things CBD, you need to have your antenna up when evaluating the claims made by the current tsunami of CBD products coming to the market. Just because they say it's so doesn't mean it's true. Consider, for instance, when a cannabis company claims that its products are organic. What does that mean? Aren't "organic" claims defined and regulated by the FDA? But the FDA has nothing to do with regulating cannabis. Because of the transitive property, how could there be "organic" claims concerning CBD products? Are there standards? Are they consistent across states? Says who? Who is policing these claims?

And don't think the FDA isn't watching claims made by these emerging CBD companies. Without clinical trials to prove their claims, many companies and their attorneys come close to crossing the line. For instance, a sleep product company I was working with couldn't claim that "it helps you sleep better." Of course, they would like to make this claim on their website and packaging, but without expensive clinical trials, studies, and proof: *no ticky, no washy.* Their lawyers made them amend their proposed packaging by stating, "*Designed* to help you sleep better." It's funny how a single word keeps you on the right side of the law. Buyer beware.

Back at Company Q, the good *doctor* also mentioned to me, with a straight face, that he envisioned that one day his magical CBD powders would evolve and ultimately cure cancer. Really? And I thought that President Obama appointed VP Biden as the Cancer Czar in January 2016!

Thousands of scientists and billions of dollars have poured into cancer research over the past century, and now this twenty-something without a degree in biology thinks he holds the cancer Rosetta-Stone in a self-formulated CBD concoction? The only other person I know of with so many potions to cure what ails us is Granny Clampett from *The Beverly Hillbillies!* Let's get real. A twenty-something dabbling with CBD isn't going to cure cancer. Only in Hooterville. In the words of *Shark Tank's* Mr. Wonderful, "Stop the madness!"

COMPANY *R:* THE BLACK BOX

You may have read about or seen a few documentaries floating around the internet and television regarding Theranos: a biotech startup founded by Elizabeth Holmes, which, at the end of 2015, was valued at $9 billion, making Ms. Holmes the youngest female billionaire ever. (***Author's note:*** She was a billionaire on paper only. Lots of things look good or work on paper. For instance, on paper, communism seems to work.)

Theranos purportedly developed blood analysis machines that would replace the need for a phlebotomist to draw a couple of vials of blood and then for labs to take days to analyze and report the results. Instead, a few drops of blood from a finger stick was fed automatically into a "black box" (about the size of a microwave). Like a frozen dinner — wait a few minutes and voilà — your results are ready.

The problem is that the technology didn't work. This was a massive fraud. But Ms. Holmes was indignant, seemingly walking around with an invisible tin foil hat which shielded her from the mind control of the real world. She, too, lived in Hooterville, only a more high-tech version, and with a better climate.

Ms. Holmes continued to raise tons of money and stacked her Board of Directors with marquee names like former Secretaries of State Henry Kissinger and George Schultz, former Secretary of Defense Bill Perry, former

Senators Bill Frist and Sam Nunn, retired Navy Admiral Gary Roughead, retired Marine Corps General James "Mad Dog" Mattis, and former CEOs Dick Kovacevich of Wells Fargo and Riley Bechtel of Bechtel. Quite an impressive list of names, which she eventually duped and who now have Theranos egg (and blood) on their faces.

None of the due diligence performed before investors poured hundreds of millions of dollars into Theranos included seeing the machine work. Ms. Holmes kept the innards of the black box off-limits to investors and most all employees. Only a small group of employees knew her dirty little secret: *the technology did not work.* A small detail, she thought. Ms. Holmes didn't let such an inconsequential problem like that stop her from continuing to raise more money. She was even invited to give a TED Talk in which she passionately explained how her technology would save thousands of lives and change the world. Her TED Talk was worthy of an Academy Award. The problem is, this female emperor had no clothes.

Are there "black boxes" in the cannabis industry? Technologies or stories that are outright invented or embellished to raise money and dupe investors, employees, and other stakeholders? You bet!

Meet Company R located in the Eastern U.S. I've become very familiar with this company that claimed to have proprietary technology to turn cannabis into water-soluble powdered cannabis that can be reconstituted with water, sparkling water, or as an active ingredient in mocktails. Many companies are developing cannabis-infused beverages or cannabis powders so that folks can drink their cannabis and mimic the social experience of alcoholic beverages. This is nothing new. Dozens of companies have products in this space. Some are better than others.

Company R, however, told investors that it had a "black box" (yes, it used those exact words), which houses many proprietary processes that make its water-soluble powders "the best" for various reasons. The reasons cited included rapid onset, complete water solubility, and the methods used don't degrade the efficaciousness and bio-availability of the multiple strains of cannabis throughout the entire process like its competitors' processes do.

One such process is a mechanical separation extraction of the trichomes, the part of the cannabis plant containing the THC. Current competing technology involves the use of extraction agents like butane and ethanol; but, the introduction of these agents into the extraction process degrades the natural "expression" of the plant. The extraction and drying process also uses heat, and heat degrades the natural cannabis product.

So, this company attempted to raise money under the guise that its "black boxes" avoid all the negatives associated with competing technologies. They gave this sample product to potential investors who were of the understanding that they derived the samples through the company's black box proprietary process. Investors were even able to speak with the company's Chief Science Officer, although not on a one-on-one basis as two of the company's founders were always present during these investment discussions to help "steer" the conversation away from potentially problematic lines of questioning. The Chief Science Officer later told me that he was counseled never to admit that the process did not work, and he was often cut off and stifled by the founders in these investor discussions. Within the company, and just like Theranos, only a few employees were in the know that one of the processes did not work as advertised in Company R's pitch decks. Like Elizabeth Holmes at Theranos, Company R's founders soldiered ahead, raising capital without fully disclosing the hole in the boat. The thought was that this was no big deal as the process would, hopefully, soon be working, even though its scientists in the lab couldn't commit to that.

As one investor, in particular, was about to commit to an eight-figure investment, Company R's CFO suddenly quit, no longer wanting to be a part of this ethically challenged management team. It's not so much that the technology didn't work, because maybe the company could get that to work in the future. It's the fact that the company's founders mislead the investor. They never came clean and said, "Just so you know, the separation technology process doesn't currently work, but we think we can get it to work by blah, blah, blah." Lack of transparency. Lack of integrity.

Upon hearing that the CFO quit, the same CFO who added credibility to the management team and someone who the investors trusted, the investor, who was about ready to write a big check to Company R, took pause. Ultimately the investor pulled out due to his unwillingness to risk his reputation by working with people lacking in integrity. Unfortunately, the cannabis industry has a disproportionate number of folks lacking in integrity. Buyer beware!

A PALACE COUP

It's a dog-eat-dog world. Families aren't immune from the cannabis industry carnage. A California-based company wasn't immune either.

Five members formed this company's Board, all of whom were related in some way, shape, or form. Pete was the CEO, chairman, and patriarch of the family. He had experience in Silicon Valley and was looking to leverage his connections in capitalizing the company. Chris was Pete's friend from other companies they worked at together and was in charge of construction for their current venture. Pete's son, Zac, and his nephew Dom were also on the Board. It was Zac and Dom who convinced Pete to put the company together in the first place and get into the cannabis business. The fifth member of the Board was Jack, who had decades-long experience growing illegal marijuana, and his "OG" (i.e., original gangster) pedigree gives this start-up cannabis company a measure of credibility with cannabis investors.

Further, Pete did not operate with integrity. He spent company funds on personal expenses. Pete's girlfriend, Teri, was not on the payroll, yet the company was paying for her Tesla SUV. Teri had Pete hire Susan, a friend of hers who, by all accounts, lacked the expertise needed for the position she was hired for.

Chris was complicit as well: big dreams, but inept with understanding what it takes to execute them. He convinced Pete to hire his wife, Jenny, in the role of Chief Compliance Officer. Her qualifications? She was a *teacher*! In this drama's Second Act, Jenny was further promoted to Chief Operating

Officer. Are these guys serious about growing a cannabis company or only interested in sucking off the corporate teat?

Time went by and the company was unable to attract an investor. Pete and Chris' self-serving actions and dubious ethics were a contributing factor. Further, their co-mingling of personal and business expenses was a source of frustration for the other Board members. With the company running on fumes, Zac, Dom, and Jack (the Three Amigos) held a clandestine meeting. They were of like minds in that Pete's grandiose vision and ego did little to move the ball forward. They did not like Pete's bullying style. They had had enough.

In what can only be described as a palace coup, the Three Amigos held a Board meeting in which they voted to fire Pete and Chris from their positions. Can you imagine how dysfunctional a company must be to result in the firing of your father and uncle?

I wonder how Thanksgiving dinner turned out.

INTERMISSION #4

KICKING THE CAN DOWN THE ROAD — REVISITING Y2K

Kicking the can down the road the way that Cannabis 2.0 companies did by selling its bag full of overpriced acquisitions to investors so that it becomes someone else's problem reminds me of the Y2K crisis in 1999.

Remember the Y2K crisis? As of 2019, we celebrated its 20th anniversary. Since the start of computer coding, programmers used a two-digit placeholder to represent the year. This is what caused the Y2K debacle. For instance, the year 1970 became "70." Programmers did this because storing every byte of data was expensive back then (hard to understand from today's perspective), so programmers took shortcuts. Everyone feared that when the clock passed midnight on December 31, 1999, the world's software would bring banking, transportation, public safety, world defense, and life as we know it to a halt. No one knew what would happen when the year "99" rolled over to "00." So, in every company and every government agency, every line of code throughout the world was scrubbed, searching for all occurrences using two-digit date logic.

The solution for the Y2K issue was to replace a two-digit date field for the year with a four-digit date field.

But my question (whimsically) remains: Isn't this the ultimate example of kicking the can down the road? In solving the immediate Y2K problem this way (i.e., by simply changing from a two-digit field for a year to a four-digit field), haven't they created one helluva *Y10K* problem?

I guess that will be someone else's problem and they'll probably begin to address this in the year 9999! Stay tuned!

DIRTY LITTLE SECRET #5

CANNABIS COMPANIES LACK DIVERSITY AND BENEVOLENCE

If you've ever reviewed a few Cannabis 2.0 company websites, you may come away with the impression that the industry workforce is diverse and genuinely charitable. For an industry with products so green, you'd expect to see a little color in its employee ranks. Not so. In short, the cannabis industry is whiter than cocaine.

Around the country, less than 3% of cannabis companies nationwide are minority-owned. In Illinois, minorities do not own any of the over eighty medical marijuana companies. Lily-white. In November 2019, the City of Chicago's Mayor (*Lori Leftfoot — I think that's her name*) held a lottery for over thirty recreational marijuana locations in the city. A photo from the news coverage went viral because it showed a room full of white men. In December, Chicago's black aldermen tried to force a vote to delay recreational weed sales in Chicago from January 1, 2020, until July 2020 because "all dispensary owners are white." One alderman told dispensary owners to "get a black partner or don't come to my ward."[32]

Anecdotally, as I've worked with a dozen or so cannabis companies, hung around numerous industry events, visited an abundance of cannabis industry operating companies, and digested multiple industry publications, media feeds, and the like, I cannot say that I've run into more than a half dozen non-white persons employed in the industry. While I'm sure some exist, I haven't seen them. And when I have run across non-white folks in the industry, they tend to be employed by vendors who service the industry (i.e., auditors, software vendors, and the like); not so much the employees of actual cannabis companies themselves.

The funny thing is that every company going public or applying for licenses touts how diverse they are. My ass! Just look at the management bios on cannabis company websites. They all look like me. Maybe a couple of women, but it's fair to say that a *lack* of diversity permeates the cannabis industry.

Recently, there is a lot of talk about social justice and proactive measures to get more cannabis license ownership in the hands of minorities. It sounds like a politically correct noble endeavor, but I'm skeptical that there is an easy solution. The deck is stacked against minority applicants as states move to adult-use and with expressed desires to fix past social injustices by trying to be minority-friendly in the license application process.

Why? First, because merit-based scoring will still give a significant edge to those with experience and already running successful operations, and those tend to be non-minority operators. For instance, Governor *Jelly Belly's* state of Illinois recently announced that applications for the next seventy-five licenses would give points for "social equity applicants" but failed to explain how many points of the total score they will award to applicants meeting the prescribed social equity applicant criteria.[33] Seemingly, minority applicants will need to partner with existing operators to bolster their chances of obtaining a license as operational experience points will almost certainly trump any points given for being a member of a "social equity" class. I'm not sure this point is thoroughly understood by these applicants.

Second, as discussed elsewhere, the cost to prepare a winning license application is in the range of several hundreds of thousands of dollars. They need to demonstrate they have lined up a capital stack of tens of millions of dollars. If they can't demonstrate the requisite financial strength, the vast majority who meet the prescribed social equity applicant criteria will be dead in the water before they put pencil to paper. (***Author's note:*** Maybe they can borrow some money from Company K's founder; after all, he's allegedly sitting on some serious cash. Just a thought.)

Thirdly, as with the State of Illinois, the time frame to complete a recreational marijuana application is too short. On October 1, 2019, they announced the plan, and just 90 days later, on January 2, 2020, the applications were due. New applicants can't put together a winning application in that short of time. In fact, this timeline works to the detriment of social equity applicants and to the benefit of entrenched non-minority license holders who have been through the application process before and who don't have to start from scratch.

As a result, I bet that the Land of Lincoln won't see too many minority applicants win licenses despite Governor *Jelly Belly's* spin on things.

COMPANY S: DIALING FOR DOLLARS

Cannabis 2.0 companies boast about how they and their employees give back to the community. But, by and large, the industry is not made up of genuinely charitable folks. They are only charitable when they need to be. And in the process of trying to score points when applying for licenses, they need to be.

Eduardo, a full-time employee at Company S, would dial for dollars, but instead of asking for money, Eduardo would call charities in states and municipalities where Company S was in the process of applying for cannabis licenses asking them if they wouldn't mind being the *recipient* of a stipend or donation of, say, $5,000 per year for the next five years. The catch? The charitable organization would agree to accept such money in exchange for Company S being allowed to use the charity's name and contact information in its license application and other marketing materials. This would hopefully demonstrate to the state that Company S is a charitable company and engaged in the community.

I've listened to these cold calls being made and often wondered what the person at the randomly picked organization on the other end of the call must have thought when they received it: "Hi. This is Eduardo from Company S. We are expanding our presence in your state, and part of our mission statement is to be a good corporate citizen. We want to give your organization $5,000 per year for the next five years if you would agree to accept our donation." Only overhearing Eduardo's side of the conversation, it seemed like 70% of the time Eduardo's spiel stopped abruptly because the person on the other end hung up on him, obviously thinking that Eduardo was part of some phone scam or the latest Jerky Boys' phone prank. Another 25% of the time, the organization on the other end of Eduardo's pot of gold cold call simply could not or did not want to get involved in receiving funds from a cannabis company. It seemed that Eduardo was successful in finding organizations willing to take Company S's money only about 5% of the time. I have never seen anybody work so hard to give away money before.

COMPANY T: THE UNITED NATIONS

To say the cannabis industry suffers from a lack of diversity is an understatement. Company T faced a lack of diversity, like the rest of the cannabis industry. Long story short: its CFO, Rich, ended up hiring a half-dozen folks from diverse backgrounds in his department that he affectionately called *the United Nations*. Here's how that unfolded.

Rich had a hard time convincing Frank and Linda, Company T's husband and wife founders, that in a sophisticated company with many legal entities, tens of millions of dollars in revenue, going through an audit for the last two fiscal years, and preparing to be a public company, that the accounting and finance departments needed more than three employees! Other public cannabis companies of similar size with founders who have real-world business experience had accounting and finance staffs in the twenty-five to thirty-five headcount range. I guess you get what you pay for: these companies with more robust accounting teams went public while Company T failed to go public, partly because it didn't have its accounting house in order.

(**Author's note:** The under-resourced Company T accounting department reminds me of my favorite story regarding the plight of under-resourced entities. When Ohio Governor John Kasich ran for President in 2016, Donald Trump accused him of contributing to the bankruptcy of Lehman Brothers, where Kasich worked. "I will say one thing about Lehman Brothers," Kasich shot back. "I ran a two-man office in Columbus, Ohio. And if I bankrupted Lehman Brothers from a two-man office, I should have been selected Pope, not run for President."[34])

The simple truth is that Company T's back office was not sufficient to support the demands of being a public company. It would take a Papal Blessing to get Company T's back office up to speed. In their decision to sell the company rather than pursue a public offering of its own, Frank and Linda left hundreds of millions of dollars of value on the table because they didn't have the back office to support the rapidly growing company. Like other inexperienced cannabis company founders, some who have already been documented earlier in this book, Frank and Linda did not know the value, let alone the need for or purpose of even the most modest level of financial infrastructure. It seemed to them that if you weren't an employee who was growing or selling the dope, you were a non-value-add cost to the business and did little for supporting top-line growth. You were viewed as a drag on profits. As such, they sought to keep those costs as low as possible.

As investors and money flowed in, various company stakeholders, of course, required financial data. Soon, the auditors had financial data demands of their own from Company T's virtually non-existing accounting department. Needless to say, the accounting department was stretched to the max. The founders soon looked foolish for not even having the most minimal level of accounting infrastructure. Unable to tread water for much longer, Rich requested, at first, and then demanded that he be authorized to hire a VP-Controller and a VP-Financial Planning and Analysis (FP&A) and about a dozen additional accountants of various experience to keep their heads above water and handle the tsunami of acquisitions that were coming down the river.

The founders were schizophrenic in their reaction to Rich's request. At times, Frank and Linda would agree to Rich's request and told him to hire these positions ASAP. Then, Rich immediately engaged with recruiters and brought in folks to interview, but when it came time to sign the offer letters for the essential Controller and FP&A positions, Frank and Linda got cold feet and told Rich that the candidates, which he and others at Company T, had spent hours finding and interviewing were not the right culture fit. Ultimately, the founders would not allow Rich to hire the much-needed help.

Company T was planning to make a move to a new office. Company T's current space, intended for twenty employees often housed thirty or more. The overcrowding at Company T's headquarters probably wouldn't pass the smell test with the local fire marshal. As part of planning for the move, Frank and Linda assigned some relatively inexperienced folks to develop headcount projections for the various departments. Rich had no input in designing the new office.

Unfortunately, as the founders began to look for a new space, they failed to understand the minimum level of corporate infrastructure that a *hyper-growth* company needs to facilitate its ability to scale. So, as the headcount planning commenced for the new office, Frank and Linda penciled in only three additional headcounts for Rich's accounting department, a department that was already severely understaffed by about fifteen positions.

Other departments also suffered from Frank and Linda's "hard-hitting analysis." For instance, the proposed new floorplan lacked privacy for departments that needed it like human resources. Employee's social security numbers, medical histories, and disciplinary actions would be in the open for everyone's consumption as there was no privacy. HIPAA violations all over the place.

All told, Company T's new office would be able to house about thirty people, only about ten more than its current location. Hardly worth the effort of moving. As the date to sign the lease for new office space that was entirely inadequate for Company T's growth drew closer, Rich commented to Frank and Linda, "It seems to me that we'll be out of space as soon as we move in."

Their sad look and slumped body language were all the communication Rich needed to affirm that they agreed with him.

So, shortly after Company T moved into its new offices, Frank asked Rich why he hadn't staffed up. "You know Rich, we have a ton of acquisitions, and we're already behind the eight ball." *Really?* When did he suddenly connect the dots? Rich had been trying to hire a dozen people since he started with the company, and hubby and wifey always vetoed him. Selective memory? Ugggh!

"So," Rich thought, "if Frank now wants more accountants, that is what he will get." Rich was not authorized to hire the key Controller and FPA positions, per Frank, just "accountants." Plain old bookkeepers, boring accountants. "Something was better than nothing," Rich thought as he was drowning and trying to keep his department's head above water, and he readily admits, he was not doing a great job at it, falling further and further behind.

In any event, to expedite a ramp up, Rich took the bull by the horns and relied on temp agencies to hire staff accountants. The next day, Rich had several interviews lined up. He figured he could get these folks in quickly, and if they worked out, he could hire them permanently down the road. After months of dyslexic leadership from Frank and Linda, Rich thought it was better to ask for forgiveness instead of permission.

Rich interviewed about ten candidates and ended up hiring folks from disparate backgrounds and different countries: Vietnam, Jordan, Croatia. He also hired an African American. A diverse bunch! Rich had the opportunity to complete a royal flush by potentially hiring a lady from Spain, but there was no more room at the inn. Nonetheless, in only two days, Rich single-handedly solved Company T's (lack of) diversity problem. Heck, Rich may have even solved the entire cannabis industry's diversity problem!

Rich reports that they were all great hires. They were professionals in a company desperately in need of professionals, and they were competent. They immediately helped the company move the needle and catch up to the diversity hype on its website, which was just marketing babble and not reflective of reality.

I hope that other cannabis companies look at Rich's United Nations and take note.

COMPANY U: AN INDUSTRY MOVER AND A SHAKER? — YES, JUST ASK HIM!

Company U had a founder, Joe, who was a thirty-something. Like other many other Cannabis 2.0 entrepreneurs, Joe had no experience in running businesses, being a fiduciary for shareholders, or anything other than looking out for #1: himself. I'm sure you've run into similar types. You know, one of those "after me, everyone else is #1" types; stretching the truth to make oneself look good; lacking in humility but not vanity; narcissistic.

He thought he was the industry's consummate deal-maker. He thought he was a God in the industry, *just ask him*. A little secret: anyone can make deals when you give the store away. I can do it, and you can do it. This isn't deal-making. Using "but it's a land grab" as an excuse for doing deals at any cost doesn't make him a good deal-maker, and certainly not a fiduciary of shareholders' hard-earned money.

One of the industry's trade rags' recently named Joe as one of the *Top 50 Most Influential People in the Cannabis Industry*. The list also mentioned other, truly deserving, cannabis industry all-stars and legends like Jim Belushi (who is growing pot in Oregon and is working on a new reality show, *Belushi's Farm*), Jared Stanley at Charlotte's Web, and Ben Kovler, Chairman at Green Thumb Industries.

Anyway, I'm not sure how Joe got on the list. Maybe he nominated himself. But his profile mentioned that he runs a charity which supports domestic-abuse prevention, women's shelters, veterans, and other fashionable causes. I reached out to him via LinkedIn and congratulated him on being on the list, in addition to being such a grand humanitarian (with his own charity no less — a regular Bill Gates). I asked, "What is the name and address of your charity so I can make a donation and support its worthy causes?" My comment was taken down — mysteriously deleted. Twice! Joe never answered my question regarding where to send a donation. I'm not sure why unless, perhaps, there was no charity to begin with. (***Author's note:*** There are many "Influential People" on this list who, based on what has happened with their companies in 2019, probably shouldn't block out their calendar for next year's awards ceremony. Like many NCAA basketball March Madness teams: one and done!)

A few months later, Joe was selected to one of those trendy "Forty under Forty" lists, popular in various cities' business magazines covering the local business scene. This time there was no mention of his charity. Did he "suspend" its operations (ala Kamala Harris' presidential campaign?)

I don't want to *charity shame* Joe or accuse him of inventing a fictitious charity for self-serving purposes, but let me take this opportunity to make a few observations about integrity.

A wise man told me that when it comes to integrity, you either have it or you don't — and you only have it once. Once you lose it, you'll never get it back. The cannabis industry is full of people who prove that the human capacity for self-aggrandizement and delusion is infinite. Saying stuff and putting words on paper doesn't make it so. Fairy dust and wishful thinking doesn't make it so. Doesn't integrity and credibility count for anything anymore?

People who have genuine integrity do what's right when no one else is watching. Doing what's right isn't doing the most convenient thing, the thing that personally enriches oneself at the expense of others, or even the easiest or least costly thing. It is doing the RIGHT thing.

INTERMISSION #5

MIRACLE ON THE HUDSON? MY ASS!

The cannabis industry is still in its incipiency, less than ten years old. The industry has gained a lot of traction since the Summer of 2018 when a ton of publicly-traded MSOs emerged. Companies like Green Thumb Industries, Acreage Holdings, Canopy Growth, Tilray, Aurora Cannabis, and the like started to make the crawls at the bottom of *Squawk Box* and *Fox Business News*. The industry has attracted a wide range of characters, starting typically with mom-and-pops, husbands and wives who took a flyer and completed state applications for dispensaries and grow/cultivation companies. These folks may or may not have any business experience.

There were and are a lot of cannabis wannabe companies not yet public all trying to differentiate themselves. Some have regional strategies (Midwest, West Coast, etc.); others have strategies only to grow or dispense cannabis.

I chuckled as I read an article about one company, Ayr Strategies, which announced that its strategy was "to acquire companies that were already profitable." What a novel idea! Although it seems like this should be an obvious goal, kudos to them. The industry needs more discipline when it comes to novel growth strategies as it migrates from its Wild West reputation to something more akin to a real industry with real investors expecting real profits.

I chuckled because somewhere in the giddiness of Cannabis 2.0 is the notion that profitability is an afterthought. Isn't that what these companies should be doing anyway? Does this deserve special congratulations from industry investors?

This reminds me of news stories which praise the efforts of the pilots of a distressed aircraft making an emergency landing: "the pilot steered his aircraft away from the residential neighborhood where he could have killed hundreds." Isn't this stating the obvious? Why is this special? Isn't this what the pilot should be doing anyway? By corollary, does that mean that the pilot of a doomed aircraft that does end up crashing into a residential neighborhood is a miscreant with an axe to grind?

Consider Captain Sullenberger who was lauded as a hero for landing an airliner on the Hudson river in 2009. Is he really a hero? I hate to be a buzzkill here, but I have a contrarian view.

His choice was binary: either crash into buildings or land on the Hudson River — much flatter, longer, and wider than any runway any pilot has ever landed on. What's the big deal? Every pilot knows the drill for loss of power: *Nose down, then trim for best glide speed (yes, all planes glide when they lose all power), and pick your best area to land. Try to restart. Communicate, "Mayday." Brief passengers.* So, he glides down and lands on the water. The plane will float a while. As a pilot, I've never understood all the fanfare about Sully. I'm not impressed. Any pilot would have done the same thing. What he did was less remarkable than the attention the media gave it. I guess it was a slow news day.

Further, I believe he should be condemned, not celebrated. Why? Because the Federal Aviation Administration has a "sterile cockpit" rule which requires pilots to refrain from non-essential activities and conversation during critical phases of flight below ten thousand feet; yet, Captain Sully, in violation of the sterile cockpit rule, is heard on the cockpit voice recorder commenting to the first officer, "Uh, what a view of the Hudson today." Hey Sully — how about a little less commentating and a bit more aviating under ten thousand feet? Maybe you could have avoided those birds, spared passengers from a dip in the Hudson, and prevented an A320 from being scrapped. (**Author's note:** When I fly, apparently unlike Sully, I have one general principle: *try to keep the number of landings equal to the number of takeoffs!*)

Still, the media and general public was looking for a feel-good story, and so they made him a folk hero, complete with a movie starring Tom Hanks, no less. A real-life, media-manufactured hero. In my opinion, Sully mythology has taken a life of its own due to the feel-good nature of the story crafted by the morning news shows. In my opinion, the myth of Sully as Hero is not deserved and is akin to the general feel-good belief that recycling is cost-effective and useful for the world, or the idea that scooter programs, popular in many cities these days, reduce the overall carbon footprint, or that paper straws replacing plastic straws will save the world. Give me a break!

DIRTY LITTLE SECRET #6

THE CANNABIS INDUSTRY IS LARGELY CASH-BASED AND SUFFERS FROM LIMITED BANKING OPTIONS

Imagine a world where:

- there is no direct deposit of your wages into your bank account. On payday, you show up at a specified time to an office without windows but with an armed security guard and a safe while the payroll manager counts your $863.74 in net wages and pays you in cash, right down to the penny;

- you tell your company's vendors to meet you and your security entourage at a secret and ever-changing meeting point so you can pay their invoice for $76,256.28 (again, in cash);

- your company pays its $27,899.43 federal monthly payroll withholding and employer matching taxes by making an appointment with the IRS. On this designated "cash collection day" (when the IRS has extra agents available to count it) you drive suitcases full of cash to the IRS offices; ditto for state payroll withholding and matching taxes;

- you deliver products to customers in unmarked vans and pick up the payment for the previous week's $18,027 delivery in cash;
- product delivery drivers routinely carry over $50,000 in cash;
- all transactions with customers are "cash only," no credit cards, and certainly no checks.

It sounds like the era where Al Capone, Bonny and Clyde, and Machine Gun Kelly thrived in the early 20th century. But this isn't the 1920s and 1930s. Instead, it is the state of the cannabis industry circa 2020.

You take things for granted every day, until they are gone — things like air, water, and a banking system. The cannabis industry suffers from a lack of banking and financial infrastructure. In the cannabis world, because the federal banking system is off-limits to plant-touching operations, companies are in constant scramble mode to execute the most basic financial transactions: pay vendors, accept payments from customers, pay their employees, finance equipment and buildings, and enter into leases.

For most dispensaries and grow facilities, the first step toward opening up for business is getting a safe — a safe that is as large as two refrigerators. Safes are designed into the architectural blueprints for both grow facilities and dispensaries. Safe companies advertise in the cannabis industry trade rags and have booths at the myriad of industry conventions. Dispensaries and cultivation centers can't function without a huge, hardened safe because most cannabis transactions accept cash only. Cannabis companies try to find cannabis-friendly state-chartered banks or private credit unions which cater to the cannabis industry. Cannabis companies' efforts to fly under the radar at traditional brand-name banks like Wells Fargo and Chase will eventually be discovered. Once discovered, their bank accounts will be closed. My advice is, "don't even try it: wastes a lot of time."

Financial institutions have various classifications for what they call Marijuana-Related Businesses (MRBs). The most restrictive MRB classification is for those companies which are plant-touching — grow centers and dispensaries. If you operate these types of companies, know that very few banks can or will want to play in this space because cannabis is a federally illegal drug. Some states have a few state-chartered private banks or private-ly-run credit unions whose Board of Directors are willing to take the risk. Cannabis companies fortunate enough to find a bank or credit union to work with them can expect usurious monthly fees. The banks claim that the huge fees they charge cannabis companies are necessary because of the extra costs involved in satisfying state regulators. (And probably just because *they can,* because the demand for cannabis industry banking services is much higher than the current supply.) Some states like Florida, Nevada, California, and more have next to no legitimate banking options.

The next level of MRBs is for businesses tangential to the plant-touching cannabis companies themselves: companies that service the industry in a vendor capacity such as companies that sell products like grow lights and fertilizers, as well as companies that provide services like payroll, audits, and the like. Many companies refuse to associate with the cannabis industry from an optics standpoint. For instance, Price Waterhouse Coopers wouldn't want to take the risk to their reputation and their relationships with their federal government clients by servicing the cannabis industry. Additionally, many potential landlords are prohibited from leasing their properties to companies engaged in unlawful activities (as stipulated by their federally insured lenders). Even non-plant-touching real estate holding companies set up for the sole purpose of collecting rent from cannabis grow centers and dispensaries are not welcome in many banks.

The most benign classification of cannabis bank accounts is for cannabis holding company checking accounts where investor money has been deposited. Theoretically, these bank accounts do nothing more than house investors' money. Banking transactions associated with plant-touching operations are not supposed to be transacted from these bank accounts. Sounds good in theory, but a *dirty little secret* is that these accounts are frequently used to transact business on behalf of the plant-touching subsidiaries of the holding company. Some banks never figure this out. Other banks don't want to figure this out, and so they look the other way.

Cannabis companies spend a lot of time trying to "trick the system." As such, cannabis company names tend to be generic in an effort to trick banks and certain vendors and not raise flags. You'll never see a cannabis company named Joe's Marijuana Dispensary, for example, but you'll see plenty of "earthy," generic-sounding company names like Joe's Healing Health Services as they try to fly under the federal banking system's radar.

Company V: Hit the bricks. Get outta my bank. Now!

Many banks will flag companies that transact business with MRBs. Once a cannabis company's account is flagged, its days at that bank are numbered.

In Illinois, the Bank of Springfield was where most of the state's cannabis companies banked. That is until April 2018 when they kicked all cannabis companies out of their bank. (Guess they couldn't take a joke anymore.) They closed all cannabis company accounts and sent their customers packing with cashier's checks for the balance in their accounts.

Fast forward eighteen months. Because some of these companies haven't found suitable replacement banks in which to stash their dough, many of these cashier's checks remain uncashed. While a few private banks have stepped up to the plate, these banks almost always limit the number of cannabis companies they want to work with at one time. While they are willing to take some risk, they all have a line that they don't want to cross over with respect to their concentration of credits in the cannabis industry.

In another example, Company V was the ultimate parent company (i.e., the holding company) of the dispensaries and cultivation centers it owned. Company V had a bank account in which tens of millions of dollars of investor money was deposited. The bank, however, restricted Company V from using that checking account for any of its plant-touching subsidiaries' transactions. Company V's numerous cultivation centers and dispensaries were stymied: they did not have checking accounts from which to write checks to pay their vendors' invoices.

The company devised a solution to set up a separate company with its own checking account. The account was set up under a non-descript name,

ABC Vendor Management Company, at a large national banking institution by one of Company V's Board members. They used this account to pay invoices on behalf of all of Company V's operating businesses. And so, for a while, ABC Vendor Management Company's bank had no idea that they would use the account to pay plant-touching cannabis industry vendors. (Is this money-laundering? Not sure.)

To prime the pump, Company V's CFO deposited a check for $50,000 from Company V's Holding Company bank account into the ABC Vendor Management Company account. The $50,000 check cleared the bank, and ABC Vendor Management Company began to write checks on behalf of Company V's operating companies to pay invoices from their various vendors.

A month later, Company V's CFO deposited a larger check to fund the checking account to pay more vendors. This time the check was $100,000. Three weeks go by, and so far, so good. Checks were being sent out of the ABC Vendor Management Company checking account to pay the various vendors of Company V's unbanked subsidiaries. Feeling bold and still with a lot of invoices to pay, Company V's CFO increased his bet yet again and deposited a $250,000 check from Company V into the ABC Vendor Management Company account. This time Company V's CFO deposited it at one of the branches of the bank used by ABC Vendor Management Company, which happened to be at Las Vegas McCarran airport while he was passing through on his way to the 2018 MJ Bizcon convention, the cannabis industry's largest tradeshow. Upon receiving the $250,000 check for deposit at the airport branch, a teller called her supervisor, and they asked some prying questions. She wanted to know the relationship between Company V and ABC Vendor Management Company. Clearly, the pattern of repeated large deposits was now on the bank's radar. The CFO nervously waited, wondering what the delay was. After about fifteen minutes, the teller's manager finally deposited the check and gave the CFO the deposit slip.

It appears that Company V's CFO pushed his luck too far because only two weeks later, ABC Vendor Management Company received a letter at its corporate offices from the megabank advising that it had one month to remove its funds from the bank as they were closing the account. The letter was stern, stating that the bank conducted an investigation, and their decision was final. The CFO thought, "*What — my money isn't good enough for you here anymore?*" The megabank never specified a reason; I guess they didn't have to. I guess they couldn't take a joke anymore.

While it isn't pleasant to get kicked out of banks (it's an administrative headache), it is prevalent in the cannabis industry. Most cannabis companies have been kicked out of banks before. A badge of honor of sorts. It seems that if a cannabis company hasn't been kicked out of a bank, that it isn't trying hard enough. Even if they already have a checking account, most all cannabis companies constantly apply to get new business checking accounts as insurance should their existing bank's Board of Directors decide that *the juice ain't worth the squeeze* in banking cannabis companies. It is a cat and mouse game, for sure.

And the banks don't stop with just kicking cannabis companies out; they also kick out the beneficial owners who established or are signers on the business account. Worse yet, banks will sometimes flag or close the *personal* accounts of innocent employees who are cashing expense checks or paychecks. Try explaining that to the wife!

COMPANY *W:* RUNNING THE FLEA-FLICKER

It was rumored that a prominent national payroll processor would not process payroll for plant-touching cannabis companies, so many cannabis companies had to run a trick play. Located on the West Coast, Company W established a payroll services company from which to pay all of its plant-touching employees at two dispensaries and one cultivation center. Trying to keep a low profile, Company W's newly established payroll services company had a generic alphabet soup sounding name: ABC Staffing. What bank is going to connect the dots that ABC Staffing is a front for paying about sixty employees at its plant-touching cannabis businesses?

Tricking the bank is step one. Company W also had to trick the payroll service provider which might stop processing the weekly payroll if it found out that Company W was actually a cannabis company. Company W feared that if the payroll provider delivered the weekly payroll to the physical location, that they would eventually find out that it was providing payroll for plant-touching cannabis companies. To stay under the radar, ABC Staffing had the weekly payroll delivered to a PO Box, instead of the actual physical locations of the operating companies. Problem solved, but a lot of hoops to jump through. Perhaps one day, with the passing of the SAFE Act (See the Company X story below), this silliness will stop.

Company X: Alternative Banking

To service the underbanked states and companies, a cottage industry of "alternative" banking has sprung up. Dozens of firms advertise that they act as a bank, offering an account number and a routing number allowing cannabis companies to transact its banking business in a typical fashion. I've investigated several such alternative banking firms, and none worked as advertised. I wasted a lot of time only to find out they were useless to me.

One such alternative banking company promised plant-touching Company X's CFO a solution for the lack of banking in Nevada. They told the CFO they said they could get Company X a bank account and a routing number, debit cards, and checks for all of Company X's Nevada subsidiaries. Their fee was steep: 2% of deposits. This means that the annual banking expense for a company with $6 million of revenue would be $120,000! Put that in your pipe and smoke it! However, five months after Company X was "accepted" by this alternative banking firm, they still never delivered on their promises: no bank account, no routing number, no debit card. Nothing, just crickets. A waste of time. This story should sound familiar to hundreds of other cannabis companies that have also tried, in vain, to find alternative banking solutions.

Currently, there is an effort in the U.S. Congress to offer banking services to the cannabis industry. The SAFE (Secure and Fair Enforcement) Banking Act of 2019 was introduced in the House and passed to the Senate. The Bill would prohibit a federal banking regulator from penalizing a depository institution for providing banking resources to legitimate mari-juana-related businesses. Among the reasons for the SAFE Act is the safety of the employees in the industry: from the drivers driving around with tens of thousands of dollars in cash to the employees who walk around with hun-dreds and even thousands of dollars in cash on payday. With all that is going on in our nation's capital, it's anyone's guess if or when the SAFE Banking Act will become law.

INTERMISSION #6

BITCOIN AND THE $80 MILLION PIZZA

In Cannabis 2.0, I've heard many entrepreneurs say, "We'll just pay in stock — it's only Monopoly money." When I hear this, it gives me pause. It gives me chills. And if you're a potential investor and hear this from your cannabis company's C-suite, then you should *run, run — run for the hills.*

As a classically trained MBA from one of the finest graduate schools of business, after the financial irrationality that occurred during the Dot. com bubble, I promised never to let my guard down again. The first step in any valuation analysis is actually to value the company; the second step is to decide how to pay for it. These are separate steps and should not be conflated. The value is the value regardless of how it is paid. Because you don't have to write a check and pay in cash, it is easy to believe that stock is Monopoly money, and in Q3 and Q4 of 2018, entrepreneurs thought that because the cannabis industry was a land grab, that all bets were off. Pay whatever it takes to acquire a company. And they did.

Would you pay $75,000 for a car worth $50,000? That's what auto salespeople try to get you to do. When they size you up, one of their first questions is, "What do you want your monthly payments to be?" Consumers end up negotiating a monthly payment instead of negotiating the price of the car. Big mistake. This is basic stuff, Finance 101. But yet, new and used car dealers encounter folks every day who focus on the monthly payment and disregard the interest rate and number of months in the finance contract that turn a $50,000 car into a $75,000 investment (and one that is undoubtedly underwater after four or five years as the remaining payments exceed the market value of the vehicle).

Hopefully, the CEOs of the cannabis companies you consider investing in don't treat their (i.e., your) stock as Monopoly money. Overpaying for acquisitions eventually dilutes all shareholders. Not bad if you can get in and out of a transaction quickly and leave the next wave of consolidators holding the bag. Unfortunately, cannabis industry stock prices as of 2020 Q1 reflect exuberant, inexpert management teams wasting a ton of shareholder value in the acquisitions they consummated thus far.

In some ways, this reminds me of the first Bitcoin transaction ever. In May 2010, 10,000 Bitcoins were used to pay to purchase two large pizzas from a Papa John's in Florida. At the time, these 10,000 Bitcoins were worth $41 to pay for $20 or so of pizza. *After all, it was just Monopoly money.* The thing is if they hadn't treated those 10,000 Bitcoins like Monopoly money, but instead, they had held onto them for about five years, those Bitcoins would have been worth *$80 million* at the peak of the recent Bitcoin valuation in 2018. That's a lotta dough for a little slice of dough: effectively, $20 of pizza ended up costing $80 million!

DIRTY LITTLE SECRET #7

SCAMMERS ARE TARGETING CANNABIS COMPANIES — *AND THEY'RE CRUSHING IT!*

Because I'm over fifty-five, I am a member of AARP. (I think it's a federal law or something.) About three or four times a year, the monthly *AARP Magazine* warns us old folks (you know, the kind who suffer from severe osteoarthritis) about common scams perpetrated on senior citizens who are ripe targets for such scams.

What's funny is that many of these scams also target cannabis companies. Why? In many respects, these companies are as feeble-minded as we portray many of our senior citizens — and with good reason. Scammers know that almost all of today's cannabis companies lack basic internal controls and corporate governance. Additionally, cannabis company employees are swamped, keeping the day-to-day operations running and, in general, trying to keep their heads above water. These factors, combined with the fact that cannabis companies are cash-rich, make them excellent candidates for theft from robbers with guns to scammers with phones and computers.

I've encountered fraudsters before. Back in the Dot.com era, I was a CFO with a fast-moving company financial services start-up. Our main product was a VISA® sponsored prepaid debit card. Kind of like PayPal (except

PayPal got it right and we went belly-up). It didn't take me long to alert the team that our losses from fraudsters were more than our total revenues. Not a recipe for success. Doesn't leave much money left to make payroll and other expenses, eh?

Here are a few of the horror stories regarding scams and insider fraud I've come across in Cannabis 2.0.

COMPANY Y: THE TRIPLE PLAY OF SCAMS, ALL IN ONE YEAR

E-Check fraud

Upon reconciling one of about twenty checking accounts at Company Y, one of the staff accountants let the CFO know about a check that he suspected had been altered. The company originally made Check number 1351 out to "Vendor A" for $2,500, but it had cleared the bank for $6,500 to an unknown recipient, and not Vendor A. As the company viewed the check image from the bank's online portal, it was easy to see that the font of the dollar amount and the payee was different from the rest of the check. Someone had digitally altered the check.

This was one of the widespread "e-check fraud" scams. The scammer somehow obtained access to Company Y's routing and bank account number and an electronic image of a typical check. The perpetrator may have done this by hacking either the company or the bank or by having an image of one of Company Y's checks, complete with a valid signature. The scammer then electronically edited the image of Company Y's checks and electronically deposited it in a bank account he or she previously set up. The bank account that the scammer used to deposit the altered check was, likewise, set up through fraudulent means in an unsuspecting bank (most likely via the internet and not in person). By the time Company Y reconciled its bank statement, the check had cleared the scammer's account, and the scammer had emptied his bank account, and they could no longer trace it.

The CFO brought this to the bank's attention, and they ended up eating the full $6,500 cost of this fraud. A month later, Company Y experienced a similar fraud in another checking account, this time for about $9,000. The bank also made good on this theft. Because there were tens of millions in these checking accounts, Company Y executives didn't sleep well until they closed these accounts, and transferred the funds to a new account. They feared the scammer could easily strike again, only next time with a few more zeros added to the digitally edited check.

Wire-transfer fraud

Another prevalent fraud these days involves spoofed e-mails that contain bogus wire-transfer instructions. Company Y fell victim to this scam also. In this particular case, hackers infiltrated Company Y's e-mail server and identified the few people in the accounting department who prepared wire-transfers as well as the executives who approve such transfers. Then, the fraudsters sent e-mails to the employees who prepare the wire-transfers to advise that "the wiring instructions have changed" and to send money wires to a different bank account at a different bank.

Company Y seemed to have a reliable internal control in place to foil this scam because the accounting department personnel were supposed to verify all wire transfer instructions in advance by calling the intended recipient to verify the wiring instructions verbally. In the Summer of 2019, however, for whatever reason, these procedures weren't followed, and because of this temporary lapse in procedure, over $25,000 was wired to the scammers. They never recovered the funds. Is this just the cost of doing business in a quickly growing company? Or was this preventable had they followed the procedures designed to thwart this fraud? In any event, $25,000 of investor's money had vaporized into the ether.

Gift card scam

Company Y also fell prey to another common scam usually targeted at senior citizens: the gift card scam. At Company Y, one of the accounting folks received an e-mail, supposedly from Victor, the owner of Company Y. The e-mail said that "I'm in a meeting now, but please go buy $4,000 of Apple gift cards at the local CVS drugstore. I need these to hand out to employees later today." Lora, the staff accountant, immediately put on her coat and left. She came back forty-five minutes later with forty $100 Apple gift cards that she charged to the company's credit card. Then, she was further instructed by "Company Y's owner" to e-mail him the gift card code numbers found on the back of the purchased cards while he was still in a meeting.

All of this seemed legit to Lora because when she poked her head into Victor's office, she saw that Victor *was* on the phone and so she didn't interrupt him. Seeing Victor tied up on a call seemed consistent with the scammer's surreptitious e-mail, but that was pure coincidence. She proceeded to upload all the gift card numbers and sent the e-mail off to "Victor." Unfortunately, a hacker had spoofed Victor's company e-mail. Victor was unaware of what was transpiring around him. The hackers immediately drained the value from the gift cards. Lora never suspected she had been targeted as an unwitting pawn in the execution of this gift card scam. Bottom line? Another $4,000 of losses at Company Y.

COMPANY Z: INSIDER FRAUD

In the non-cannabis world, hiring is a process. Companies must plan for, budget, approve, and fill positions. They must carefully write job descriptions. The human resource department conducts a multi-tiered screening process and holds several rounds of interviews. They make background checks, do drug testing, and check references. A month or so later, the company hires a properly vetted, experienced new employee who is a good culture fit with its needs. Companies generally hire slowly and fire quickly. The hard and soft costs of not having the right butt in the right seat are profound.

The process is quite different in companies moving, seemingly, at the speed of light. Like the Dot.com era, Cannabis 2.0 companies are not so much concerned that they have the *right* butt in a seat as they are that they fill a seat by someone who will fog a mirror (i.e., someone alive; no other qualifications). No time to waste. Such was the case at Company Z, whose owners looked at things like background checks, reference checks, and a 360-degree interview process as unnecessary and unimportant. They just slowed down the hiring process. The company did not value these hiring safeguards as important gating steps to make sure they hired only the best candidates. And in the cannabis industry, it's not surprising that most companies disregard drug testing altogether.

Jill, the only bookkeeper at Company Z, was such a hire: no background checks whatsoever. Jill earned the trust of Ross, the owner, who trusted her to write checks, reconcile the bank accounts, prepare financial statements, and even sign his name to checks in case she had to cut a check and he wasn't around. Any auditor would have a field day with the lack of internal controls at this company because there was no separation of duties. This is, as they say, *bass ackwards*. With no oversight or internal controls, Jill, if she so chose, could embezzle money from the company without anyone noticing. Guess what? Jill, "so chose."

Like many other cannabis companies circa 2018 Q3, Company Z wanted to go public. The first step was getting audited financials, and the first step in getting audited financials was hiring an auditing firm. The first step for the auditing firm in determining whether or not it would audit Company Z's books was doing background checks on the owners and other key people in Company Z. Unlike Cannabis 2.0 companies that lack internal controls and processes, auditors engaged by cannabis companies have strict protocols in determining which clients they choose to do business with. They've seen it all. They are professional and prudent and won't be rushed. They are careful not to put their firms in positions in which they don't want to be. Many Cannabis 2.0 companies don't share the same concern.

So, the auditors began to do background checks on Company Z's key employees. One night, Company Z's recently hired CFO received a call from Joe, the audit partner. Joe told the CFO that in the ordinary course of qualifying Company Z as a potential client that they routinely performed background checks on Company Z officers and employees in the accounting department. They had uncovered a concern regarding Jill. Joe then proceeded to e-mail him an article they found about Jill. Complete with a mug shot of Jill, the article was a story of her conviction and serving time in prison for embezzlement in a previous job she had in another state. Shocked, the CFO shared the e-mail with Ross, Company Z's owner. Ross was equally shocked; after all, he was responsible for hiring Jill. Joe made it clear that they could not proceed with the audit of Company Z unless or until they terminate Jill. This is why non-Hootervillian companies take the time to perform background checks on all hires.

The problem is that because Ross, like other cannabis company founders, never worked in corporate environments before, he devalued the accounting function and skimped on staffing this department. As such, Jill was on the critical path of almost every transaction for the past two years for Company Z. Ross knew that without Jill, there would be no audit, and without an audit, Company Z couldn't go public. Quite the conundrum indeed, but this was an unforced error caused by Ross's lack of effort in developing a sound hiring process.

Ross struggled with what to do. Ordinarily, he would show Jill the door immediately, and others in the accounting department's bench would suck it up until they could hire and train a permanent replacement. The problem is that Company Z had no bench strength in the accounting department. Like almost every Chicago Bears team since 1985, Company Z's depth chart was void of additional players. Ross determined that the best solution was to terminate Jill as an employee but keep her on as a contractor for the time being. A cosmetic fix for sure, but one that the auditors accepted.

Ross confronted Jill with her past, and she cried as she explained that she was the breadwinner in her family, and had to take money from her previous employer, but would never do the same here at Company Z. Jill groveled, begged forgiveness, and understood to continue to do work for the company that she would do so as a contractor and not an employee. She promised to be on her best behavior.

Ross relayed the particulars of the new arrangement with Jill to Company Z's CFO. The CFO asked Ross, "Do you know that as a contractor, Jill will no longer be eligible for company benefits?" Ross said that he discussed that with Jill, and she understood. This arrangement was tenuous as the CFO needed additional resources, redundancy, and internal controls in the accounting department. Like knowing the Globetrotters always prevail against the Generals, the CFO had an uneasy feeling of how this story would end.

Ross needed to build some bench strength immediately to make up for years of neglect in the accounting department. The CFO was finally able to convince Ross of the need for additional staffing.

So, for the next few months, Jill was on a short leash and seemed to be on her best behavior. After a few months, however, the CFO uncovered some irregularities:

- Company Z's monthly group insurance invoice for health coverage showed it was still paying over $1,000 per month for Jill's and her family's benefits;
- The company's credit card showed numerous unidentified purchases from Amazon that were delivered to an Amazon locker in another state;
- The CFO reviewed the contractor invoices that Jill submitted and determined that Jill submitted more invoices than for those to which she was entitled.

Upon digging deeper, the CFO asked the bank for a copy of several of the checks that Jill cashed while as a contractor. He determined that she had forged his signature on several checks she prepared. Jill was at it again. She had embezzled another $20,000 in the course of a few months! The auditors' due diligence processes in identifying Jill as a potential internal control risk were spot on.

The company hired additional resources a few months prior, so all of Company Z's accounting eggs weren't in Jill's basket anymore, and they were in a much better position to terminate her as a contractor. Because Jill still had a lot of institutional knowledge that they needed during the audit, it would still be difficult with her gone, but the impact on the audit and the company would now be minimal.

On a Friday, the CFO tactfully suggested to Jill that she may have made some mistakes in her invoices to the company and asked Jill her to reconcile her invoices and payments received and report her findings on Monday. Of course, by this time, the CFO knew the extent of the embezzlement and that this was not an innocent mistake. He knew that this would back her into a corner, and the jig was up. On Monday, when Jill came in, he asked to see her reconciliation of invoices to the company. Out of excuses and painted into a corner, she said she left her reconciliation at home. (i.e., The dog ate her homework!) The CFO asked Jill if she remembered the results of her reconciliation. Jill, trying to minimize her "mistake," said, "Yes. You know, as it turned out, you were correct. I inadvertently submitted two more invoices than I should have." The CFO had given her just enough rope to hang herself before he put the hammer down and presented her with the evidence. He showed her his reconciliation, which detailed that she had paid herself some ten weeks more than she earned and also showed her the forged checks she had signed in pulling off this fraud. When confronted with this evidence, there wasn't a lot that Jill could say.

The meeting ended when the CFO suggested that the company no longer needed her services. Without protest, Jill gathered her personal effects, and was escorted out the door. That is the last Company Z heard from Jill. In a final act of mercy, Ross chose not to involve the authorities.

And so these stories of scams and frauds perpetrated on just a few cannabis companies are representative of what happens when internal controls are lacking or subverted, when the wrong butts are in the seats, and when owners do not understand or value investing in the administrative and back-office functions that will allow their companies to scale.

INTERMISSION #7

THE BULLSHIT GENERATOR

My favorite website from the Dot.com days was *bullshitgenerator.com*. It is "Google-like" in its simplicity. It is still around today. Check it out.

The website's stated purpose:

> *This tool is dedicated to generating bullshit for your next meeting, proposal, interview, conversation with your boss, whatever.*[35]

I first used this valuable tool in the Dot.com days when I was preparing PowerPoint pitch decks for investors and internal presentations. A simple press of the Bullshit Generator's red *GENERATE BULLSHIT* button will randomly generate all sorts of marketing double-speak in phrases that make it look like you know what you're talking about. Some samples:

- *Monetize virtual initiatives*
- *Matrix proactive markets*
- *Utilize seamless convergence*
- *Transform global deliverables*
- *Synthesize extensible markets*
- *Target value-added paradigms*

- *and more!*

I thought this website died when the Dot.com bubble burst, but it is back up and running and generating bullshit in a verb-adjective-noun format that is tailor-made for cannabis company CEOs and their marketing teams. Imagine how much better and effective cannabis pitch decks could be if the marketing folks used the *Bullshit Generator* to punch up their company's presentations. They could come up with valuable bullshit like:

- *Co-mingle state-specific licenses*
- *Engage geo-specific cannabis customers*
- *Deploy quality edibles branding*
- *Enable cross-media product lines*
- *Disintermediate front-end dispensary consultants*
- *Aggregate 24/365 initiatives*
- *and more!*

While the *Bullshit Generator* is not proprietary to the cannabis industry, there's another tool solely dedicated to calling "bullshit" in the cannabis industry: check out *The CannaBS Detector Podcast.*[36] I have a feeling that this podcast is going to be very busy in 2020.

It seems like no matter the era or industry; there is always a need to generate bullshit for many occasions. The cannabis industry is no exception.

CONCLUSIONS AND PREDICTIONS

As predicted, and right on cue, November 2019 proved apocalyptic for cannabis companies' earnings reports. The rapture began on Thursday, November 14, when Canopy Growth announced revenue that fell well short of analysts' estimates. Similarly, another Cannabis 2.0 bellwether, Aurora Cannabis, reported sequential double-digit revenue percentage *growth,* but at the same time, its net income percentage *declines.* (What's wrong with this formula for success?) Aurora Cannabis was out of control. Its stock immediately tanked, plummeting about 17% on November 15, 2019 (the next day), the largest single-day percentage decline for Aurora shares in more than five years and closing at its lowest price since October 2018."[37] A stock analyst noted, "possible cash pressures (are) evident."[38] That is a tactful way of saying that the ship is sinking — and fast! Clearly, as of 2019 Q4, the markets don't care about top-line revenue growth from failed land grab strategies anymore. They demand immediate bottom-line profitability. Cannabis 2.0 companies' survival depends on it. By November 18, only four days later, the vultures were out: at least one law firm wants to speak with investors who have suffered losses in Aurora Cannabis securities to contact them as they open an investigation for misleading financial reporting and disclosures.

These *Black Thursday* (Is it too early to coin the phrase "Black Thursday?" *Too soon?*) announcements took the entire cannabis sector's stock prices even further down. One must wonder how much deeper this elevator shaft is.

REFLECTIONS AND LEARNINGS OF CANNABIS 2.0

As we begin a new decade in 2020, I reflect on my learnings and observations in the spectacle that is Cannabis 2.0:

- Just as with the Dot.com era, the Cannabis 2.0 industry is not immune to the immutable laws of traditional finance. Never bet against them. Bubbles will burst. Valuations will return to the equilibrium as determined by the rational laws of finance and not by loud voices from the carnival barkers occupying cannabis company C-suites;

- Acquiring companies at *any* cost without understanding fundamental financial underpinnings that govern financial transactions is not sustainable. A land grab mentality will fail without experience at the helm imparting discipline in allocating limited resources;

- The proverbial *smartest guys in the room* are not currently occupying the C-suites of Cannabis 2.0 companies, although *they* think they are;

- Decision making based on "gut" and wishful thinking (emotional decision making) rather than decisions based on objective data and financial analysis (intellectual, fact-based decision making) is a root cause for the predicament in which the Cannabis 2.0 industry finds itself;

- Milquetoast, inexperienced Cannabis 2.0 Boards of Directors have given a hall pass to management's greed, naïveté, and dearth of transparency, integrity, and ethics;

- The value of stock options for many industry employees are underwater. Employment in the industry, while still attractive, is not the panacea it was less than a year ago;

- California, arguably one of the largest cannabis ecosystems in the world, is mired in an inexplicable mix of legal and illegal weed growers. California's investment environment will remain toxic until the illegal growers are put out of business;
- Greedy states and municipalities which rushed out and imposed high taxes on their marijuana programs only added fuel to the black market for marijuana. As a result, the long-term tax revenues from their marijuana programs will actually be reduced and not maximized. Economics 101: Supply and Demand.

So, welcome to the shit show, the circus that is the cannabis industry circa 2020 Q1. Unfortunately, it's not getting better anytime soon. We're already seeing previously announced mega-blockbuster acquisitions unravel and other indicators of an industry seemingly in freefall. Consider:

- In October 2018, MedMen announced the acquisition of PharmaCann in an all-stock deal valued at $682 million. A year later (almost to the day) the deal was scuttled, MedMen's U.S. tracking stock which was trading as high as nearly $7 a share in October 2018 is trading at less than $.25 as of February 2020;
- In conjunction with announcing *underwhelming* 2019 Q3 results, Harvest Health and Recreation announced it is scaling back its previously announced purchase of cannabis licenses from CannaPharmacy, Inc. priced initially at $88 million in an all-cash deal;
- The $850 million acquisition of Verano Holdings by Harvest Health and Recreation (announced March 2019) that was initially targeted to close by June 2019 is still not closed as of February 2020. If the deal ends up closing, it looks like it will be with Harvest's stock trading at about one-third of the price than when it was first announced;
- As of February 2020, one of the most significant exchange-traded funds (ETF) tracking the cannabis industry (trading under the

symbol MJ) is trading at less than half its value less than one year prior;

- An oversupply of THC and hemp in Canada and many U.S. states are causing prices to tank, not even covering the cost of production;

- Numerous cannabis industry venture and private equity funds, which, as recent as 2019 Q3, were still raising their second, third, and fourth funds to put new bets out on the cannabis roulette table, are now hunkered down. Instead of investing in new cannabis industry companies, they are reserving any remaining or new capital for the anticipated additional cash needs of their existing portfolio companies, which generally are not cash flowing and burning through cash.

To say that the industry has gotten out over its skis is putting it mildly. Continuing the metaphor, will this industry be able to course-correct in the air and land safely on the snow at the bottom of the ski jump hill, or will it end horribly in a crash like Vinko Bogataj, the "Agony of Defeat" guy?"[39] A trusted managing director of a prominent cannabis-focused private equity firm summed it up best when he told me: "Good luck out there; it's getting ugly fast."

LOOKING AHEAD TO CANNABIS 3.0

So, what's next for the cannabis industry? Only a few years old, and in many respects, already an old maid at the dance. The race to go public in 2018 was almost singularly focused on Multi-State Operators doing a land grab. It was the same story over and over, ad nauseum. All of the pitch decks and public offering circulars resonated with the same tired themes. They all had the same maps showing their footprints of dispensaries, grow facilities, and production facilities, just with different pins marking different geographic territories. Their executive management biography sections tried to prop up inexperienced founders as industry visionaries. How could all companies claim to have *the best* management team, strategy, operations, products, and locations?

If they were all "the best" then why were they all trading at near all-time lows as of February 2020?

The music has stopped in this game of musical chairs for MSOs. Their glory days are in the rearview mirror, and they'll stay there for quite some time. The well of unlimited capital has run dry, and so the Cannabis 2.0 Ponzi scheme won't work anymore.

Looking forward, the cannabis industry can expect that:

- companies will need to put on their big-boy pants and get real in managing their dwindling cash through downsizing, canceling expansion plans, and operating the company as a going concern with limited resources;

- more companies will restate previously issued financial statements and take goodwill and asset write-offs, resulting in further reductions in earnings per share;

- cannabis and stock market regulators will continue to investigate companies leading to more shareholder litigation;

- investors' investment thesis' will transform back from simply putting bets out on the roulette table hoping that one of their investments hits it big to making disciplined investments with battle-tested management teams;

- Boards of Directors will hold their management accountable, and many additional Cannabis 2.0 executives will be shown the door;

- investments in MSOs will be out of favor for a few years until they regain the trust of the investment community through:
    * replacing inexperienced management,
    * meeting their projections and analyst guidance, and
    * fully integrating the disparate companies that they have already acquired;

  Be patient. This could take a while, and cannabis stocks will continue to be volatile;

- investment focus will move away from MSOs and to some areas on the fringes of the cannabis industry that show investment promise:

* CBD cigarettes,
* THC and CBD-infused beverages,
* water-soluble CBD and THC powders,
* consumption lounges,
* and more;

- current supply and demand imbalances in some states and Canada will eventually reach equilibrium through further industry consolidation, stricter enforcement putting illegal grows out of business, bankruptcies, better management, and more strategic marketing;
- distressed cannabis assets will be scooped up for pennies on the dollar;
- real-estate investment trusts (REITs) will gain favor, buying existing cannabis cultivation centers in sales-leaseback arrangements, providing a much-needed, albeit one-time, cash infusion to many Cannabis 2.0 companies;
- the SAFE Act will be enacted in advance of full federal marijuana legalization, and this easing of banking regulations will allow companies to bank and borrow money in a typical fashion, adding much needed financial lubrication to aid in the growth and safety of the industry;
- major pharma, tobacco and alcohol companies, looking for another sin to sell, will continue to make investments in the industry; this will be viewed favorably by the financial markets because these companies will bring discipline to the industry as well as enhance industry valuations by offering attractive Cannabis 3.0 exit opportunities;
- federal legalization will occur within the next five years, at which time cannabis companies will also benefit from a) access to U.S. equity markets and unparalleled liquidity for their securities, and b) the ability to transport products across state lines, as opposed to the current separation of operations by state. This will, in turn, add invaluable efficiencies in production, marketing, branding, and

distribution, and it will set the table for genuine national brands with marketing power fueling brand awareness.

Time will tell. Check back in a few years.

DON'T FALL IN LOVE WITH A DREAMER

Life is full of dreamers. Cannabis 2.0 is full of dreamers. Visionaries are dreamers with unlimited resources. It's easy to be a dreamer, but it's another thing to understand that resources are not unlimited. Resources need to be managed and allocated. Cannabis 2.0 does not view resources as scarce; instead, they are squandered and wasted. Not all dreamers have the skills and maturity needed to be excellent operators capable of executing a strategy, scaling a company, and acting as a fiduciary for stakeholders other than for oneself. These dreamers' marijuana-pipe dreams have turned into nightmares as access to capital has gone from ridiculously easy to all but shut off. Cannabis 3.0 companies will need to survive (or not) on their own cash flows; that is, of course, if they have any at all.

Reality has now caught up with companies like MedMen and its inexperienced executive dreamers who now find themselves in unchartered waters, scared, and desperate. They appear only to have enough cash to last until 2020 Q3. There's chum in the water, and the sharks are circling. This is bad news for MedMen shareholders for sure. They are not alone. The days of reckoning in the cannabis industry have begun in earnest. It's going to get worse before it gets better.

All I can say to Adam, Andrew, and the hundreds of lawyers, donut shop owners, and others who, despite not having relevant experience, somehow found their way into Cannabis 2.0's C-suites and key management positions, and who fancy themselves as self-proclaimed Cannabis 2.0 visionaries: "Take a knee. Pass the baton and turn the keys over to folks capable enough to fix the problems you created in Cannabis 2.0.

You're no Bradley Jacobs."

INTERMISSION #8

SIX SIGMA?

I was once in the international airline catering industry. Pretty basic stuff — putting food on airplanes for a captive audience. I worked for a $200 million, privately-held company. The owner, Sue, was an interesting woman and a true entrepreneur. She built this company from nothing, figuring it out as she went along.

As a member of her Senior Leadership Team, she called me into her office, and she told me about an article she read on Six Sigma. I had previously learned about Six Sigma in business school. It is a set of techniques and tools for process improvement, which was developed by Bill Smith, an engineer at Motorola. Jack Welch incorporated Six Sigma into General Electric. Through these tools, controls, and processes, it is 99.99966% statistically expected that these parts or processes will be free of defects.

Sue asked if we should implement Six Sigma at our international airline catering company. My thought was: "Six Sigma? Who does she think we are? General Fucking Electric? How about starting with One Sigma? You know — basic blocking and tackling. Yeah, let's start there."

Because the company was already losing $6 million per year on $200 million of revenue, we had bigger issues than Six Sigma could address. We had fundamental people, structure, and process issues to address. Let's focus on the blocking and tackling and attacking the low hanging fruit, and we'll fix 90% of the problems. Implementing Six Sigma costs millions, and for a company the size of Sue's, *the juice ain't worth the squeeze.*

Similarly, any new, hypergrowth industry like the cannabis industry should also be focusing on getting their biggest bang for their buck in the least amount of time. Cannabis 2.0 companies should concentrate on basic blocking and tackling before they think about running more sophisticated plays — no trick plays, just three yards and a cloud of dust for now.

References and Endnotes

1   *Raging Bull.* Dir. Martin Scorsese. Perf. Robert DeNiro. MGM, 1980.

2   Arcview Market Research & BDS Analytics, *The State of Legal Marijuana Markets, Excerpt,* 6th Edition, "Executive Summary," p.2; accessed December 17, 2019. https://www.bvresources.com/docs/default-source/book-excerpts/the_state_of_legal_marijuana_excerpt.pdf?sfvrsn=d8cecfb2_4.

3   Journal of the American Medical Association.

4   "What Does Gone to Pot Mean?" Writing Explained, accessed December 17, 2019. https://writingexplained.org/idiom-dictionary/gone-to-pot.

5   Steve DeAngelo, *The Cannabis Manifesto* (North Atlantic Books, 2015).

6   "Senator, you're no Jack Kennedy," Wikipedia, accessed December 17, 2019. https://en.wikipedia.org/wiki/Senator,_you%27re_no_Jack_Kennedy.

7   "Best Performing Stocks of the Decade," Seeking Alpha, December 13, 2019, accessed December 17, 2019. https://seekingalpha.com/article/4312349-best-performing-stocks-of-decade.

8   Tam Harbert, "Buyers Beware," *CFO,* September 13, 2019, p. 41.

9   Compassionate Use of Medical Cannabis Pilot Program Act, (410 ILCS 130/); January, 2014.

10 Ibid.

11 Ibid.

12 "Illinois Lottery: The Land of Lincoln Is So Broke, Lottery Winners Are Being Paid In IOUs," Inquisitr, October 15, 2015, accessed December 17, 2019. https://www.inquisitr.com/2497541/illinois-lottery-the-land-of-lincoln-is-so-broke-lottery-winners-are-being-paid-in-ious/.

13 Tom Schuba, *Chicago SunTimes,* October 24, 2019.

14 Greg Hinz, "Greg Hinz on Politics," *Crain's Chicago Business,* October 23, 2019.

15　"Naperville," Niche, accessed December 17, 2019. https://www.niche.com/places-to-live/naperville-dupage-il/reviews/.

16　Valerie Strauss, "Finally, Democratic candidates talk about education in a debate. But nobody raised this key issue.", The Washington Post, September 15, 2019, accessed December 17, 2019. https://www.washingtonpost.com/education/2019/09/15/finally-democratic-candidates-talk-about-education-debate-nobody-raised-this-key-issue/.

17　Kevin LaCroix, The D&O Diary, November 25, 2019, accessed December 17, 2019. https://www.dandodiary.com/2019/11/articles/securities-litigation/a-rash-of-cannabis-related-securities-class-action-lawsuits/.

18　*Scooby Doo.* AOL-Time Warner, Turner Broadcasting Division.

19　*Animal House.* Dir. John Landis. Perf. Tom Hulce. Universal Pictures, 1978.

20　Statue of Liberty Inscription, 1903.

21　Stephen Rodrick, "Rise of Big Weed: MedMen's Growing Pains," *Rolling Stone,* April 16, 2019.

22　"Meet Andrew Modlin of MedMen in Culver City," Voyage LA, January 30, 2017, accessed December 17, 2019, http://voyagela.com/interview/meet-andrew-modlin-medmen-headquartered-culver-city/.

23　"MedMen Announces Layoffs and Overall Plan to Achieve Positive EBITDA," MedMen Enterprises, Inc., Press Release, 11/15/2019, accessed December 17, 2019.

24　Complaint for Damages, Superior Court of California County of Los Angeles, James Parker (MenMen ex-CFO) Plaintiff v. MM Enterprises USA, LLC, et al; filed January 29, 2019.

25　*Forrest Gump.* Dir. Robert Zemeckis. Perf. Tom Hanks. Paramount Pictures, 1994.

26　Ibid.

27　*Caddyshack.* Dir. Harold Ramis. Perf. Bill Murray. Orion Pictures, 1980.

28　*The Simpsons.* "The Cartridge Family." Dir. Pete Michels. Perf. Nancy Cartwright. Gracie Films; FOX Broadcasting Company and 21st Century Fox. Season 9, Episode 5, November 2, 1997.

29　Compassionate Use of Medical Cannabis Pilot Program Act, (410 ILCS 130/); January, 2014.

30　Referral from Independent Counsel Kenneth W. Starr in Conformity with the Requirement of Title 28, United States Code, Section 595; September 9, 1998; Footnote 1128.

31   Hagens Berman, PRNewswire, November 18, 2019.

32   "Will Legal Weed Be Delayed? Black Aldermen Force A Vote Next Week Because All Dispensary Owners Are White," Block Club Chicago, accessed December 17, 2019. https://blockclubchicago.org/2019/12/13/will-legal-weed-be-delayed-black-alderman-force-a-vote-next-week-because-all-dispen-sary-owners-are-white/.

33   "IDFPR Announces Next Round of Adult Use Cannabis License Appli-cations," Illinois Department of Financial and Professional Regulation, Press Release, October 1, 2019, accessed December 17, 2019. https://www.idfpr.com/News/2019/10%2001%202019%20Conditional%20Adult%20Use%20Cannabis%20license%20application%20Release.pdf.

34   Kailani Koenig, "John Kasich: "I'm Going to Be the Republican Nominee After We Win Ohio'," NBCNEWS, March 12, 2016, accessed December 17, 2019. https://www.nbcnews.com/politics/2016-election/john-kasich-i-m-going-be-republican-nominee-after-we-n537116.

35   www.bullshitgenerator.com, accessed December 17, 2019.

36   "The CannaBS Detector," Tunein, accessed December 17, 2019. https://tunein.com/podcasts/Business--Economics-Podcasts/The-CannaBS-Detec-tor-p1151027/.

37   Hagens Berman, PRNewswire, November 18, 2019.

38   Ibid.

39   "The Agony of Defeat Guy," The Medical Questions, November 16, 2013, accessed December 17, 2019. http://www.themedicalquestions.com/articles/the-agony-of-defeat-guy.html.

About the Author

Having earned an MBA from the #1 MBA-Finance program in the country (University of Chicago), a BS-Accountancy from the perennial #1 undergraduate accounting program in the country (University of Illinois), and a CPA, Dean Matt has seen it all in over thirty years in the C-suite.

In his latest adventure, Dean came out of retirement for a unique opportunity as a CFO for a multi-state cannabis industry company. Eight short months later, that company was sold for almost *$1 billion* in what was at the time *the largest transaction in the history of the U.S. cannabis industry.* To date, he has worked with about a dozen companies in the industry.

Dean has served as Chief Financial Officer, Chief Operating Officer, Controller, and in Mergers & Acquisitions positions from start-ups to Fortune 100 companies in and privately-held, private equity-backed, and publicly-held environments. Dean has taken companies public, endured bankruptcies, survived the Dot.com bubble, uncovered Ponzi schemes sending executives to prison, and has helped engineer many successful exits, netting shareholders billions. He has worked for world-class entrepreneurs such as Bradley Jacobs (United Waste Systems, United Rentals, XPO Logistics) and Wayne Huizenga (Waste Management, Auto Nation USA, Blockbuster Video, Boston Market, Extended Stay America, Republic Waste, and more).

Dean's storytelling ability was honed and recognized at a young age, winning awards from the National College of Teachers of English and Gwendolyn Brooks, Illinois' Poet Laureate. He also hosted a reality TV show pilot for a travel and golf-themed show called *The Grass is Greener.*

Dean's passions include bad golf (since grade school) and safe flying (since high school). Dean and his wife look forward to one day returning to their retirement, running their golf accessories business (www.golfgear.golf), and resuming their golfing/traveling lifestyle (www.mucho-dean-aero.com).